WHER
YOUR BUDDHA
NATURE?

WHERE IS YOUR BUDDHA NATURE?

STORIES
TO
INSTRUCT
AND INSPIRE

By Master Hsing Yun

Translated by Tom Graham

First edition, 2000

Published by Weatherhill, Inc.
41 Monroe Turnpike, Trumbull, Connecticut 06611

Printed in the United States.

Library of Congress Cataloging-in-Publication Data:
Hsing-yün-ta-shih.
Where is your Buddha nature? : stories to instruct and inspire/by Master Hsing Yun;
translated by Tom Graham.
p. cm.
ISBN 0–8348–0449–2
1. Religious life–Buddhism. 2. Buddhism–Anecdotes. I. Graham, Tom. II. Title.

BQ5405 . H65 2000
294.3'4432–dc21   00-022560

TABLE OF CONTENTS

INTRODUCTION

The best way to introduce a story teller is to tell a story about him. One day Master Hsing Yun was attending to the day's business in a small conference room. A group of ochre-robed monks and nuns was helping him by recording his decisions and preparing them to be transmitted to the right places. The monastic organization that Master Hsing Yun oversees is very large and nearly every decision he makes affects a lot of people. Needless to say, not everybody is always happy with everything he decides. Decisions, by their very nature, discourage some as they encourage others. At one point, when a particularly difficult judgment was called for, Master Hsing Yun raised his head to take in the room. When those in attendance saw him pause and look around, they drew near to him for they could see the deep concern in his eyes. At last he spoke. "Do you understand why the Buddha is revered by so many people?" His eyes indicated a statue of the Buddha set in a wall nearby. "Do you understand why he is worshiped in so many parts of the world?"

His question clearly called for no answer. The group looked first at the statue of the Buddha and then at Master Hsing Yun as they waited for him to continue.

"It is because he never speaks. He just sits there and never says anything to anyone."

As his small audience struggled to control its laughter, Master Hsing Yun continued. "And me?" he said, "All I ever do is talk and that's why I have so many problems!"

Master Hsing Yun, whose name means "star cloud," is a large man. He has the arms and chest of a someone who was used to heavy labor when he was young. His head is closely shaved in the traditional style of a Chinese monk. Though he has experienced health problems in recent years, his voice and manner are steady. His followers describe him as being boylike, for he carries himself with an innocence that seems to be remembered from a childhood spent in the countryside. Western Jiangsu, the part of China that he is from, is known for its poverty, its agricultural products, and its tradition of storytelling. People from that part of China are good

9

speakers, distinguished by their pluck and their ability to be self-effacing when standing before large groups.

The story above was told to me by someone who heard it from someone else. A few incidents I remember from my own experience show other sides of him. Once a small group of us was visiting the future site of Hsi Lai University near Los Angeles when we were accosted by a man who seemed to take great offense at our being where we were. The man shouted so loudly and carried on for so long that we were forced to leave the room in which we had been sitting. As Master Hsing Yun walked past him, I watched to see what his reaction would be. As the angry man shouted at him just a few inches from his face, he showed no sign that anything was happening at all. He made no move to defend himself or to look at his antagonist. When we regrouped outside of the building, he made no mention of the incident. As we stood in the parking lot, his years of ascetic training were fully apparent, for he had managed to completely remove himself from the tension of his surroundings. While the rest of us glanced back at the man still shouting in the doorway, Master Hsing Yun seemed to have entered a silent and deeper part of his being.

On another occasion that I witnessed, he traveled for over two hours to speak to an American disciple who had been disturbed by the Al Gore fund-raising incident that had taken place at the temple in Hacienda Heights. Master Hsing Yun explained what had happened, why it had happened, and apologized liberally for any misunderstanding that may have resulted from his actions. I thought that his humanity and humility were impressive. The man who was disturbed by the incident, probably because he could not understand Chinese, continued to be disturbed by it and eventually left the temple, despite the master's apology to him.

It is hard for Westerners, who are so used to laws and abstractions, to achieve what Dostoyevsky called "in-feeling" for the ways of other societies, in this case the ways of a Chinese monastery. There are rules in the monastery, but the most important rule is always the master himself. His decisions and his actions determine the tone of everything that happens. In the secular sphere, this kind of system may lead to the abuse of the governed, but in the religious sphere, it more often leads to a massive burden being placed on the shoulders of the one who governs. The head of a monastery is called a "master" in English, a word that inspires fear and rebellion. Westerners always see the obeisance that is demanded of the student in this relationship, but they rarely see anything more. In Chinese, the master of a monastery is called "teacher-father." While it is true that a "teacher-father" should be respected, it is also just as true that he must expend all of his energies on his disciples.

The stories in this collection will give readers a fascinating view into the mind of one of China's great modern teacher-fathers. Some of these tales concern life in the monastery or events from Chinese history. Some of them are autobiographical and some of them are concerned with the lives of his disciples. All of them are told with deep feeling.

In the autobiographical section we are given glimpses of his boyhood, his early years as a monk, and the hardship he endured when he first arrived in Taiwan. We are also given many insights into the qualities that allowed him to build the largest Chinese monastery in the world today. Readers may be surprised to learn that his success is built much more upon kindness and concern for his followers than it is upon determination, though of course, there was much of that too. In his stories about his disciples, we learn how he thinks about his followers and how he understands his responsibilities to them. In the stories about monastics and Ch'an masters, we see how other Buddhist monks and nuns have reacted to situations in their lives.

To my eye, the most interesting element in this collection is seeing how Master Hsing Yun thinks of others. Anthropologists call the "teacher-father" relationship a "fictive kin" relationship because it draws on the primal energies of the family. This seems like a loaded term to me because it implies that there is something false about the relationship. It seems to say that we are fooling ourselves if we look elsewhere for the love and security we ideally experienced in our families when we were children. In the West, this may be true, who knows? While all of us have many teachers, few of us have teacher-fathers who really help us climb to new levels of achievement and self-awareness. We are even strained in English to come up with a word for people like that. We call them mentors after the name of Odysseus' tutor,

Mentor, or we call them coaches in a feeble attempt to expand sports into a metaphor for life. A teacher-father is someone who accepts us into the greater family of his mind. In the stories in this collection, we see this side of Master HsingYun, and we see it from many different angles. I believe that his perspective on his responsibilities for those who call him teacher-father makes for some very powerful reading, and I would ask readers to watch their own reactions as this aspect of his personality appears on the page. Who, besides your mother or father, thinks that way about you? And isn't this how we all should be thinking about each other, as much as we can.

Incidentally, nuns are also called "teacher-fathers" in Chinese, for this relationship is understood as being as fully maternal as it is paternal. Indeed, the Buddha himself, who is the greatest teacher-father of all, is a manifestation of a transcendental reality that both includes and surpasses all gender distinctions, as well as all other conceivable opposites.

Though the essence of a good story lies in its drama and emotion, the Buddhist ideas of compassion and generosity play a very important role in this collection. It might be helpful to say something about them here. Buddhists use the word *compassion* rather than love because for them the word love traditionally connoted what might be called "clinging love," the kind that can make us jealous. The Buddha described compassion as meaning "what a mother feels for her child." It connotes profound empathy and concern for other beings. It is based on a deep intuitive understanding that all living beings are one, and that what is good for one of them is good for all of them.

The word *generosity* also has different connotations in Buddhism than it does in English. In a Buddhist context it means something more like "profound sharing within the recognition that we all are Buddhas." Generosity is the basic urge to reach out to others and help them. The Buddha taught that there are three fundamental kinds of generosity: material generosity, emotional generosity, and the generosity of sharing wisdom with others. The purpose of each of these kinds of generosity is to free others from suffering and fear. The Buddha often described emotional generosity as the generosity of "making others feel unafraid," for he knew very well what it feels like to be a conscious being with an impermanent body in a dangerous world.

In addition to the dynamics of the teacher-father relationship, readers will also find that the ideas of compassion and generosity inform nearly all of these stories on many different levels. They are central to all of Buddhism, as well as to the toil of teacher-fathers, whose primary goal is to attract people to the truth.

Master Hsing Yun is the forty-eighth patriarch in the Lin Chi (Rinzai) line of Chinese teacher-fathers. Master Lin Chi (?-867) is famous for his apparently outrageous statements. He is the one who once yelled, "If Shakyamuni Buddha came around today and started preaching the Dharma, I'd beat him to death with a stick and feed his body to the dogs!" He also once said, "What use is the Tripitaka? Bring it here and I'll use it as a rag!" The Tripitaka is the officially recognized and (normally) revered collection of Buddhist sutras and commentaries. Master Lin Chi's outrageous statements were not meant to offend us, but to open our minds to a world of truth that lies beyond reverence and beyond formal religious practice. If you can hear the compassion in his voice as it echoes through the centuries, you will have understood an essential part of Ch'an Buddhism. If you feel empowered and a little less afraid of your world because of his statements, you will have understood another part of that great tradition. The Ch'an lineage began when the Buddha handed a flower to Mahakashyapa. The flower signified that the core of the Buddha's teachings had been successfully transmitted "mind to mind" to his disciple.

Master Hsing Yun often says that he is a Buddhist teacher-father and not a Ch'an one. He does this to overcome lingering divisions that still exist within the Buddhist community, and probably also to distance himself a little from the eccentric image of Master Lin Chi. China is still a conservative society and projecting a wild image is simply not going to bring very many people into the temple. Master Hsing Yun has become a major force in the revitalization of modern Chinese Buddhism precisely because he has brought millions of people into the temple. He has followers in nearly every country in the world. At the heart of his teachings is the explicit message of the importance of human life and the need for compassion in everything that we do.

I think there is also an implicit message delivered by Master Hsing Yun wherever he goes, and this is a message of courage and inspiration that has little to do with the words he speaks or writes. In the spirit of Ch'an this message must be received directly into the mind. Whenever I visit him I am as impressed by his wonderful sense of daring as I am by his compassion. The quality in him that people describe as innocent or boylike also seems to be ancient, something that has been handed down from one generation to the next during the twenty-five centuries that have intervened since the Buddha gave his flower to Mahakashyapa. The Buddha gave him the flower because Mahakashyapa had smiled at something the Buddha had said. I bet that Master Lin Chi also gave something extraordinary to those of his disciples who laughed at his jokes. I know that Master Hsing Yun has something to give us, too. I hope that readers will find it in this collection of tales.

TOM GRAHAM

WHERE IS YOUR BUDDHA NATURE?

THE
BUDDHA

THE BUDDHA'S SENSE OF EQUALITY

One day, the Buddha went for a walk with Ananda. When the two reached the outskirts of Shravasti city, they saw an untouchable coming toward them carrying a bucket full of excrement.

The untouchable, whose name was Nidhi, saw the Buddha and Ananda at the same time they saw him. Deep in his heart, Nidhi had immense reverence and love for the Buddha. However, he also had very little respect for himself, and thus he believed that he was completely unworthy of the Buddha's attention. Though Nidhi loved the Buddha very much, when he saw that he was coming his way, he turned down a side road to avoid meeting him. The Buddha knew what Nidhi was feeling and why he wanted to avoid him, so he asked Ananda to continue walking straight ahead while he followed another path that would lead him right to the untouchable.

When Nidhi saw that his attempt to avoid the Buddha had failed and that the Buddha was coming straight toward him, he turned this way and that, looking for some last place to conceal himself. In his confusion, his bucket of excrement tipped over and the foul slop spilled across the road. By the time Nidhi had realized what he had done, the Buddha was so close to him, he could no longer even attempt to run and hide. All he could do was kneel by the mess, press his palms together, and say, "Buddha! I am sorry!"

With great gentleness, the Buddha said, "Nidhi, please stand up."

When Nidhi heard him say that, he stayed on his knees and wondered, "How can he know my name? I never would have imagined the Buddha would ever call me by my name!"

The Buddha continued speaking, "Nidhi, will you come and be one of my monks?"

Nidhi was shocked by what he thought he had heard. He said, "I am a low and filthy person, and I am not good enough to be one of your monks. I know your monks are all of the warrior and Brahmin castes. I am not good enough to be among people like that!"

The Buddha only smiled when he heard Nidhi say that. Then he said, "Nidhi, we don't think like that at all. My Dharma is like clean water. It can wash the defilements away from anyone and anything. My Dharma is like fire, and it can burn away all ignorance. My Dharma is like the ocean, which can hold anything in it. Among us monks, there is no distinction between class or caste, high or low, better or worse. All such distinctions are the merest illusions.

"Even our bodies are mere illusions. With wisdom alone will we learn to see beyond them. Free yourself from delusion, Nidhi, and come with me now."

By the time the Buddha was finished speaking, Nidhi was so moved that he agreed to cast away his old life and follow the Dharma with the Buddha and his Sangha.

SWEEP AND CLEAN

One day, while the Buddha was walking past the door of the monks' quarters, he heard Ksudrapanthaka sobbing loudly. Near him, a circle of monks had gathered to laugh at him for being so foolish. The Buddha approached Ksudrapanthaka and asked him why he was crying.

"What has made you cry so hard?" he asked.

"Oh, Buddha," he said, "I am just a stupid person. I followed my brother into monastic life, but I seem to be unable to remember anything I am taught. My brother has tried to teach me the Dharma many times, but I always forget what he tells me. Today he told me that since I have such a bad memory, I should leave the monastery and go back home. Oh, Buddha! I don't want to leave. Please help me!"

When he was finished speaking, the Buddha replied very softly, "Don't worry about how much you know or don't know. That's not important. It is a form of wisdom to realize that one is ignorant, and it is a form of igno-rance to believe one is wise. Come with me now."

Following this exchange, the Buddha began spending extra time with Ksudrapanthaka. He began to teach him to repeat the phrase, "Sweep and clean, sweep and clean." Ksudrapanthaka, however, proved unable to remember even these simple words. When the other monks learned of this, they decided that Ksudrapanthaka was beyond all hope. The Buddha, how-ever, continued to be compassionate with him, and he continued trying to teach him the phrase.

"Take this broom," the Buddha said to him. "As you sweep the grounds, say the words I have taught you over and over again."

Ksudrapanthaka did as Buddha told him, but the other monks were not happy with the way he wandered around with his broom all day mumbling to himself. They said he was disturbing them and told him to stop what he was doing.

When the Buddha heard what they had said to Ksudrapanthaka, he told the monks that he had expressly told Ksudrapanthaka to do as he had been doing and that they should not interfere with him in any way.

After the Buddha spoke to them, the other monks began to feel concerned about Ksudrapanthaka and they all tried to help him memorize the phrase the Buddha had asked him to learn, "Sweep and clean, sweep and clean."

With the added support of the other monks, Ksudrapanthaka was able to try even harder to learn the phrase the Buddha had taught him. He worked at it day after day until he was able to say it without any help from anyone. Then, slowly, he began to really think about the words as he swept back and forth across the grounds of the monastery. He thought to himself, "There are really two things that must be swept and cleaned. One of them is outside and the other is inside. The dirt and dust outside of us is easy to clean away, but the dust and dirt inside of us requires great wisdom to clean away. The dirt and dust inside of us is nothing other than our suffering, our greed, our anger and our selfishness."

Ksudrapanthaka continued sweeping and he continued thinking. And as he continued, his mind gradually started becoming brighter. Things he had been unable to understand before gradually became understandable to him.

He thought, "All of the dust inside of human beings originally is caused by only one thing: desire. Only wisdom can overcome desire. If desire is not overcome, then the cycle of birth and death cannot be escaped and suffering can never end. Desire causes suffering and it causes karma, which keeps us lashed to the wheel of birth and death. As long as we are victims of our own desires, we can never be free.

"As soon as we rid ourselves of all desire, however, our minds will be pure. We will see the truth and we will be free forever."

As Ksudrapanthaka continued sweeping and thinking like that, he slowly managed to clean his mind of all its impurities. Gradually, he entered a state of complete equanimity wherein he had neither desires nor aversions, wherein he saw neither good nor evil, and wherein all his previous ignorance was entirely eradicated.

Ksudrapanthaka became enlightened.

With his new understanding, he went joyfully to the Buddha and said, "Buddha! I am liberated! I have swept and cleaned just as you told me, and by doing so I have swept away all the impurities in my mind!"

The Buddha was full of joy to hear what Ksudrapanthaka had said, and from that day on, Ksudrapanthaka became one of the Buddha's most respected disciples. Even still, Ksudrapanthaka did not change his usual routine. Every day after that he could still be seen slowly sweeping the grounds of the monastery as he chanted softly to himself, "Sweep and clean, sweep and clean."

BREAKING THE PRECEPTS
TO SAVE A LIFE

During the life of Shakyamuni Buddha, Queen Mallika of Kosala became a devout Buddhist. She took the vows of a Buddhist to not kill, not steal, not lie, not engage in sexual misconduct, and not abuse her senses with intoxicants. Since Queen Mallika was so kind and compassionate that she was loved deeply by the people in her kingdom.

One day, while Queen Mallika was in the middle of an important

Buddhist retreat, she heard that King Prasenajit was going to execute his cook because the cook had offended him. When she heard what the king was going to do, she invited him to come to her chambers for a feast.

She prepared a great meal with all the king's favorite foods, including an abundance of alcohol and meat. She also made sure that the man who cooked the food was none other than the cook the king was planning to execute.

When King Prasenajit came that night, he was pleased with what she had prepared for him, but he was also curious as to why she had done it.

He said, "You usually never drink alcohol or eat meat. On top of that, you are in the middle of an important Buddhist retreat. Why have you gone to all this trouble just to break your vows? And why are you doing it today of all days?"

Queen Mallika answered, "I heard that you were angry at your cook and were planning to have him executed. If I didn't have him cook this one last meal for me, I was afraid I might never again be able to taste food as good as this."

When the king heard what she had said, he realized that his anger was out of proportion to the offense the cook had committed. He also realized that due to a minor flaring of his own temper, he had almost killed someone who was of real value to him. On the spot, he canceled the cook's execution, and from that day on the king was much more thoughtful when he made decisions.

TWO BEGGING BOWLS

After their meal, the monks settled into a slow, walking meditation, as was their usual custom. One of them, however, seemed unduly concerned about something.

The Buddha asked him, "Is something bothering you? You appear to be troubled by something."

"Buddha," the young monk replied, "someone gave me a very beautiful begging bowl. I want to give the bowl to Ananda, but Ananda is away and he won't be back for seven days. It's one of your rules that no monk should possess two begging bowls for more than one day. I just don't know what to do."

The Buddha was exceptionally sensitive to human feelings and human affections, so on the spot, he announced to everyone that henceforth monks would be allowed to possess two begging bowls for as long as one week at a time.

By changing his rule like that, the Buddha's showed both his affection for Ananda and his concern for the monk who wanted to give Ananda the bowl. Whenever problems arose, the Buddha always found a solution that made everyone happy.

TWO ROBES

Upali was clearheaded and fairminded, and for this reason, the Buddha often asked him to help resolve differences of opinion that sometimes developed within the monastic community.

One hot summer, in the midst of the summer retreat period, a controversy developed within one of the Buddha's monastic communities. Since the monks in that community were unable to resolve their conflict among themselves, the Buddha asked Upali to go there and help them solve the problem. The community Buddha wanted him to go to was in the state of Shachih.

When Buddha asked Upali to go, Upali did not want to refuse his request, but he also felt more than a little unwilling to go to Shachih. He said to Buddha, "Buddha! Please see if you can find someone else to go there to resolve this problem!"

"Why are you unwilling to go?" the Buddha asked when he heard Upali's words.

"Oh, Buddha! Shachih is a long way from here and it often rains there. According to our monastic rules, I can only have one robe with me at a time. If I get caught in the rain, and my robe is soaked, it will take a long time to dry and I will not be able to collect my thoughts or work effectively once I am there."

The Buddha thought for a moment and then asked, "How long will the whole trip to Shachih take you?"

"It will take two days to walk there," Upali said. "Then it will take at least two days to settle the controversy, and then it will take two more days to come back. The whole trip will take six days in all."

When Upali had finished speaking, the Buddha called everyone together and announced that from then on, during the summer retreat season, monks would be permitted to possess two robes for as long as six days at a time.

CARRYING HIS FATHER'S COFFIN

One day, while the Buddha was in the hills meditating, a messenger came from his father's palace to tell him that his father was ill. The Buddha quickly settled matters in the monastery, and went to see his father.

When his father, who was ninety-three years old, saw that his son had returned to see him, tears filled his eyes as he stretched out his hand to greet him. The Buddha stepped forward to grasp his father's hand. Around them, the ministers and officials of his father's kingdom all wept openly and with real feeling.

When King Suddhodana saw their grief, he said, "Don't feel sad for me. There is nothing to be sad about. All living things in this world must die. I am completely satisfied with my life, and now that my son is here I am ready to pass on. My son became the Buddha, and from that I have derived untold comfort and joy. Now that I am blessed with this one last sight of him before I die, I feel as if I already have seen the brilliant radiance and glory that follows upon death of the physical form."

As soon as he stopped speaking, the king smiled slightly and pressed his palms together. Then he died.

That night, as custom dictated, a group of men sat beside the king's body as it lay in its coffin. The Buddha, Nanda, Ananda, and Rahula were among the men who were present in the room. At one point, Nanda, who was the Buddha's half-brother, said to the Buddha, "When the coffin is carried to the funeral pyre tomorrow, please let me be one of the bearers."

When Ananda and Rahula heard Nanda say that, they both asked if they could be pallbearers, too.

The Buddha assented to all of their requests. Then he said, "And I will be a pall bearer in the funeral as well."

The next day, the king's funeral procession was exceptionally dignified and magnificent. People from all over the kingdom lined the roadsides on their knees, weeping openly. When they saw that the Buddha himself was acting as one of the pall bearers for his father's coffin as it proceeded toward its pyre, they were moved beyond all words and beyond all expression. All they could do was bow in reverence and respect at the sight.

CARING FOR THE ILL

During the time of the Buddha, there were two monks who usually were sent to visit people who were ill. One of the monks was an old man who had been a monk for many years. The other monk was a young man who had not been a monk for very long.

People were always grateful to be visited by a monk, but as time went by, they began to realize that there was a big difference between which monk they were visited by. Those who had been visited by the old monk quickly got well, while those who had been visited by the young monk usually got worse. In addition to that, people who had been visited by the old monk usually became very happy, while those who had been visited by the young monk became sad.

Eventually people figured out that what the monks were saying during their visits was very different.

The young monk would say, "Life is short and full of suffering. Illness is the result of bad karma from the past catching up to us. There is nothing you can do about it, and there is no cure to be had."

The old monk would say, "All phenomena are transient. Nothing lasts for very long. Your illness will disappear quickly if you spend some extra time chanting the Buddha's name and reflecting on how to be an even better person once you are well again."

When Buddha heard this story, he was full of praise for the old monk, and he instructed the young monk to spend more time studying with the old man.

HIGHER LOVE

During the time of the Buddha, there was a young
monk who saw a young woman every day when he went to her village with
his bowl to beg for food. The young woman's face was beautiful and her
eyes were clear, and as the young monk saw her day after day, the two of
them began to fall silently in love with one another.

Before long, the young monk could not bear his desires any more. He
went to Buddha, fell to his knees, pressed his palms together, and said in a
voice heavy with grief, "Oh, Buddha! I am suffering with love! Her beautiful face and piercing eyes follow me wherever I go. I feel as if she is watching me all through the day. I can think of nothing but her, and therefore I
am no longer able to practice and meditate as I should. I beg you to let me
leave the monastery because I must marry this girl or I will die!"

The Buddha listened quietly to the young man. He observed his agony,
but said nothing about it. With immense kindness and understanding he said
to him, "If you are certain that you want to leave the monastery, you may do
so immediately. You have my blessing for that. However, if you have any doubt
about your decision, I would ask you to remain with us for three more days."

The young monk was deeply moved by the Buddha's obvious compassion and wisdom. He thought about how peaceful and harmonious life in
the monastery was. His passion for the girl in the village was strong, but it
would be possible, he decided, to remain in the monastery for three more
days as the Buddha had suggested.

To be sure the young man would comprehend the full meaning of his
decision to leave, the Buddha scheduled three days of meditating on the
nine unclean aspects of a dead body. The young monk participated dili-
gently in the meditating and chanting for three full days without ceasing.

At the end of the last day, the Buddha went to the monk's room. When
the monk saw him, he bowed before him and exclaimed with great joy,
"Oh, great Buddha! Thank you! My desires have lost their hold on me. I
never want to leave this place again! Your teaching has shown me where my
desires would lead me in the end."

PRACTICE
IS LIKE TUNING A STRING

When Sronakotivimsa first became a monk, he was very enthusiastic. He was so enthusiastic, in fact, he expended too much energy trying to improve himself. As a result, he became tired of Buddhism. The path seemed long, and as Sronakotivimsa assessed himself, he decided it was more than he could do. He had to quit.

He felt ashamed of himself, but he saw no other option than to go to the Buddha and explain that he was going to have to leave the monastery because he was just not able to go on.

Sronakotivimsa expected that Buddha would criticize him for his decision, so he was surprised when Buddha only spoke to him with great kindness and understanding.

He said, "What was your profession before you became a monk?"

Sronakotivimsa replied, "I was a musician. I played the sitar."

The Buddha looked at Sronakotivimsa for a moment and then said, "If a sitar string is tuned too tightly, what will happen when you start to play?"

Sronakotivimsa answered, "The string will break."

"If the string is tuned too loosely," the Buddha asked, "what will happen then?"

"If the string is too loose, you will not be able to play anything," Sronakotivimsa replied.

"There you have it, Sronakotivimsa," the Buddha said, as he smiled with great consideration and understanding. "Practicing the Dharma is just like tuning a string on a sitar. If we practice with too much intensity, it is just as if we had tuned a string too tightly. It will break easily. Conversely, if we are lax in our practice and let the days slip by without doing anything to improve ourselves, then it is as if we had tuned our string too loosely. Nothing much will come of our meager labors.

"Up until now you have been overly diligent and energetic in your practice. That is part of your nature. If you return to the world now, there is a great danger that you will continue in much the same way. You will overdo it there, too. You will very likely throw yourself into the pleasures and demands of the world and cause yourself great suffering.

"Sronakotivimsa, true practice requires that we understand how to find a balance between suffering and joy, between pleasure and pain. We need to walk the middle way between these two opposites. Can you understand that?"

"Oh!" Sronakotivimsa said as if suddenly awakened. "So practice is like tuning a string on a sitar. If you get it just right, you will be able to play beautiful music!"

After their talk, Sronakotivimsa decided to stay in the monastery. From that day forward, he made great progress in his practice.

A REPRESENTATIVE

During the Buddha's lifetime, one of his disciples was an excellent speaker who was good both at intellectual discourse and at conveying the emotion necessary for making the Dharma appealing to ordinary people. His name was Katyayana. After spending years with the Buddha, he decided to travel to southern India to preach what he had learned.

Not long after he arrived in the south, Katyayana succeeded in persuading a young man from a good family to become a monk. The young man's name was Sonakotikanna.

Once Sonakotikanna had shaved his head and begun to follow Katyayana, he heard many stories about the Buddha and how excellent and virtuous he was. Gradually a strong desire to see the Buddha in person arose in his heart. One day, Sonakotikanna learned that a group of traders was planning to travel north to do some business. He asked Katyayana if he could go with them so that he could see the Buddha for himself.

Katyayana was delighted that Sonakotikanna had developed a longing to see the Buddha, so he assented to his request immediately. Katyayana asked only that Sonakotikanna pass on his best wishes to the Buddha as soon as he got there.

After a long journey on foot, Sonakotikanna finally reached the Jeta Grove in Shravasti where the Buddha was staying. He immediately rushed to see Buddha. During the course of the conversation which ensued, Sonakotikanna passed on Katyayana's best wishes as he had promised he would do. When the Buddha learned that Sonakotikanna was Katyayana's disciple and that things were going well in the south, he was very glad. Later, he asked Ananda to put an extra bed in his room so Sonakotikanna could stay with him.

That night, the Buddha went to speak with Sonakotikanna again. He asked him many questions about his life and about any difficulties he might be having in learning the Dharma. Sonakotikanna asked Buddha five questions about the Dharma that night. The Buddha's answers were so careful and complete, they have been compiled into a sutra called the *Sutra of Sixteen Significant Things.*

The next morning, Buddha gathered all his monks together and had Sonakotikanna repeat everything they had talked about the night before. Sonakotikanna was deeply satisfied with the concern Buddha showed him. Soon after this he left to go back to the south.

After Sonakotikanna had gone, some of Buddha's monks began to grumble about his visit. They complained that Sonakotikanna was really just some nobody from far away and that Buddha should never have shown him so much respect and talked with him for so long. When Buddha heard about what some of his monks were saying, he used the opportunity of a Dharma talk to explain himself to them.

He said, "Sonakotikanna is young and he is not a great monk himself, but he was a representative from Katyayana who is preaching in the south. I have been concerned about Katyayana for a long time. When I honored Sonakotikanna, it was not just him that I was honoring. I was also honoring Katyayana and all others who preach the Dharma in distant lands."

Stories About

CH'AN
MASTERS

GETTING TO THE POINT

Ryokan was a great Japanese monk. He spent his life cultivating good behavior, while paying close attention to even the smallest of details.

One day, when he was quite old, a group of his relatives came to see him. They told him that his sister's son had developed some bad habits. They said that he was drinking and gambling, and consorting with prostitutes. Ryokan's relatives were afraid that the young man would squander all of the family's wealth if his bad behavior was not quickly brought to a halt.

They were deeply concerned, and they pleaded with Ryokan to return to their village to reason with the young man before it was too late. As the group continued its pleas, the old man concluded that he had no choice but to return to his village and do what they had asked him to do.

The village was a long way away. Ryokan walked for three days before arriving. When his nephew saw that he had suddenly come to town, he became suspicious that the family had asked the old monk to come and per-suade him to change his ways. Ryokan's nephew had not forgotten all of his manners, however, and despite his suspicions, he did remember to invite his uncle to spend the night with him at his house.

The two spent the night chatting peacefully together. Not once did Ryokan say a single word about his nephew's intemperate behavior. The old monk talked on innocently as if he had never heard that anything was the matter at all.

The next morning, when Ryokan was getting ready to leave, he asked his nephew to help him with his shoes. "I'm old," he said. "My old hands shake so much, I can't tie my own shoes. Would you be kind enough to help me?"

His nephew knelt before him to help him with his shoes. As the young man worked, the old monk said, "Thank you, thank you! When a man gets old, there is not much he can do anymore. Look, I can't even tie my own shoes. Be sure to take good care of yourself while you are young. Learn to be a good person and to make a good foundation for the day when you become old like me."

When he was finished speaking and his nephew had finished fastening his shoes, Ryokan bowed his head and slowly walked away. Not once did he say a single word about the foolish things his family had told him his nephew was doing. Nevertheless, from that day on, his nephew completely changed his ways. He stopped drinking and gambling, and he came very much to resemble his old uncle in the goodness and kindness with which he treated everyone he met.

THE TEARS OF A MASTER

One day, Master Kuya was traveling through the countryside on foot when he was suddenly ambushed by a group of thieves brandishing knives. As the thieves drew nearer to Master Kuya, they could see that he was beginning to weep. One of them started laughing at the sight of a Buddhist monk crying like that.

"What a useless monk you must be," he said, laughing with contempt. "A monk is not supposed to be afraid to die!"

Kuya replied, "Oh, I am not afraid to die at all. I am only crying because I know that you are throwing your whole life away by doing these evil deeds. You think you are gaining by stealing from others, but really you are only losing everything of value by throwing your own goodness on the side of the road. If you kill me, it won't matter much at all to me, but it will matter to you. You will get such terrible karma for your evil ways, I don't know how many eons you will spend in hell."

As the thieves listened to Master Kuya speak through his tears, they realized that he was telling the truth and that he really was weeping only for them. When they understood how vast his compassion was, they resolved to change their ways immediately. Not long after that, they all took refuge in Buddhism under Kuya himself.

NOT FOR THE SAKE OF ANGER

Ch'an Master Chin Tai loved orchids. Whenever he had free time, he would tend his orchids. He had a room full of hundreds of plants of many different varieties and colors. Everybody knew how important they were to him.

One day, Master Chin Tai had some business to take care of away from the monastery. He asked two of his disciples to watch over his orchids for him while he was gone. The two were fully aware of how much Chin Tai loved his plants, so they made sure to be especially conscientious in the performance of their duties. They made sure to check the greenhouse several times a day, and they made sure they watered the orchids in exactly the way Master Chin Tai had asked them to.

Unfortunately, one of the two was a little too fastidious in the way he treated the Master's plants. As he watered one of them, he paid so much attention to the flow of water going into the plant that he forgot what was happening with the back of his watering can. In a moment, he accidentally pushed a whole rack of flowers over.

After the crash, all he could see was the ground scattered with broken pots and the fallen forms of Master Chin Tai's precious plants. The disciple was new to the monastery, and he was afraid that he was going to get into serious trouble when the Master found out what he had done.

With a sharp sense of dread, he cleaned up the mess on the floor as he waited for Master Chin Tai to return. When Chin Tai came back that night, the disciple threw himself on the ground in front of him and begged his forgiveness.

Chin Tai listened to the disciple and from his words he could tell that the young man was deeply afraid that he would become angry with him. To allay his fears as well as to teach him something valuable, the Master said, "Young man, I grow orchids only as an offering of beauty to the Buddha.

"You don't need to ask my forgiveness because you have done nothing that needs to be forgiven. I do not grow orchids to bring anger and fear into the world.

"People should be like orchids. We should bring beauty and joy into the world. Don't be afraid of me, and don't ever again feel that you should be afraid of anyone."

OVER THE WALL

Master Sengai took many young monks into his monastery for training. These young monks were really just boys, and many of them were not yet past the age when play and mischief were far more attractive than discipline and study.

At night, groups of them sometimes climbed over the monastery wall, not returning until quite late. They used a tall, wooden stool to help them sneak over the wall.

One night, Master Sengai saw their wooden stool in the shadow of the corner of the wall where the young monks had left it. He removed the stool, and then waited until he could hear them coming back. As he heard them start to climb over the wall, Master Sengai crouched with his hands on his knees exactly where the stool had been.

As the young monks came over the wall one after the other, they each in turn found themselves surprised, then immensely subdued, by the fact that the hard stool they were accustomed to had turned into the soft shoulders of their master.

The boys waited in silence until the last of them had descended. Prepared for anything, they were surprised once again by the simplicity of their master. He was as gentle as could be as he patted them on their backs and said, "It's cold tonight! Please hurry back and put on some more clothes to keep yourselves warm!"

Master Sengai never mentioned the incident again, but after that night, his young monks never climbed over the monastery wall again.

Master Sengai handled this matter beautifully. He instructed the boys without humiliating them or damaging their self-esteem. He taught them the right way to behave by taking extra time to show them that he really cared.

All parents should stop and think this way the next time they want to influence their children.

BORROWING FROM BUDDHA

Master Chi Li was an accomplished and devout Ch'an master. After a day of preaching the Dharma and chanting sutras, he wanted nothing more than to settle down in Buddha Hall before the altar to meditate all night long.

Very late one night, as Master Chi Li was meditating, a thief slowly pushed open the large wooden doors of the hall. The thief could see a form sitting in the shadows before the altar, but when the form did not move, he concluded that it must be someone sleeping. "If I am quiet," he thought to himself, "I'll be able to slip right by him without him ever knowing a thing."

The thief then proceeded to move stealthily through the shadows toward the donation box in front of the altar. He took the money in the box and slowly backed out of the temple. Just as he was starting to slip through the large doors again, Master Chi Li spoke up.

"Wait a minute!" he said.

The thief was surprised to hear the sudden sound of a voice and paused in mid-step.

"You have forgotten to thank the Buddha for the money you took," Master Chi Li said, without moving from his meditation posture.

Without thinking, the thief said, "Thank you!" before running away through the doors.

A few days later, the thief showed up at the temple again. This time he was escorted by a policeman who wanted to check on his story. It seems that the thief had robbed a few other places nearby and that, finally, he had been caught. In jail, he had also confessed to stealing money from the donation box in Master Chi Li's temple.

When Master Chi Li heard this story he said, "No, no. He did not steal anything here. It didn't happen like that at all."

WHERE IS YOUR BUDDHA NATURE?

The policeman said, "Master, don't try to protect him! He broke the law and he has confessed to it himself!"

"Is that what he said?" Master Chi Li responded. "I do remember seeing him here a few days ago. He did take some money, but he was borrowing the money, not stealing it. I am sure of this because he said 'Thank you' to the Buddha before leaving. If you don't believe me, you can ask him if that's not true."

The thief was still punished for his crimes, but after he was free to go his own way again, he returned to the temple to apologize for what he had done. In the end, he was so moved by the kindness and tolerance of the Zen master that he decided to become a Buddhist himself. He remained to study in the same temple from which he had stolen the money.

MASTER IKKYU SUNS HIS SUTRA

A crowd climbed Mount Hiei. In the temple above, nuns were placing damp sutras in the sun.

Master Ikkyu let them climb the hill. He knew they believed that they would be healed and made wise by breezes that had passed over the sutras.

"Why don't I sun my sutra?" Ikkyu asked. Then he took off his clothes and lay in the sun.

Many in the crowd who climbed the mountain saw him and were shocked at his nudity. A group of monks from the temple above rushed down the hill to speak to him. "You cannot do this now," the monks said. "You must not act like this here."

Ikkyu looked at them and replied, "The sutras you are sunning in the monastery are dead and have worms. The sutra I am sunning is alive. It can preach the Dharma. Why is it you don't know which is more valuable?"

I HAVE A TONGUE, TOO!

When Master Kuang decided to study Ch'an, he went to Master Chen first. He was put to work in the kitchen during the day. At night he chanted Buddhist sutras to improve his character.

One day Master Chen came by and asked, "Which sutra are you chanting now?"

Kuang answered, "*The Lotus Sutra.*"

Without pause, Master Chen said, "If the sutra is here now, where is the lotus?"

Kuang did not know. "Please tell me where it is."

Master Chen again was direct. "No, I cannot tell you. No one can tell you that," he said.

Kuang felt humiliated by their exchange. A short time later, he left the monastery. He wandered far and wide across vast China, but his wounded pride went with him everywhere. He visited over fifty different teachers but still he could not attain enlightenment.

One day he found a new teacher from Hunan, Master Shoushan.

Kuang asked him, "What can I do? All around me I see the treasure and I hear it, but I can not feel it. I can not realize it."

Master Shoushan said, "You can touch what is outside only by what is inside."

Suddenly Kuang was enlightened. Then he said, "Now I understand what tongues these Ch'an masters have in their mouths!"

"Yes?" Shoushan asked.

Kuang said, "Now I understand that I have a tongue, too. That is all."

Shoushan was delighted with this reply. "You truly have realized the heart of Ch'an," he said.

THE MASTER BECOMES A SON-IN-LAW

Master Ikkyu was a free-spirited monk who was as compassionate as he was insightful and independent in his views.

One day, he went to the home of one of his disciples only to find the man and his wife deep in sorrow. Ikkyu asked them what the problem was. The two told him, through their sobs, that their business had collapsed and that they no longer were able to pay their debts.

"We have nothing left," they said, "and no place to hide. Our friends avoid us because they don't want to lend us money, and our creditors hound us day and night. There is nothing left for us to do, except kill ourselves."

"There is always a solution to every problem," Ikkyu said.

"Not this time," the couple replied. "All our possessions have been sold and we have nothing left!"

"Is there not even anyone left in your family?" Ikkyu asked, trying to assess the fullness of the problem.

"We have a daughter, but she is only thirteen years old. If she were a little older, we would be able to marry her to a wealthy man and save ourselves, but thirteen is still too young."

"That's not a bad idea," the Master said. "Thirteen is not too young. Marry the girl to me!"

When they heard him say this, the two were not sure if he were joking or serious. They said, "Master, don't make a joke out of this! She's just a girl! And anyway, you are a monk. How can a monk get married?"

Very seriously Master Ikkyu replied, "As far as I can see, there is no other hope for you two but this. Quickly prepare the announcement and invite everyone to come to the wedding as soon as possible!"

On the day of the wedding, many, many people came to watch the monk marry the child. Master Ikkyu sat in the front room of the house behind a table on which there were many Chinese fans. The master was writing short poems and signing the fans. He said, "Anyone who wants to see the wedding must buy a fan. One dollar per fan."

No one objected to the price, which was quite low for the calligraphy of a famous monk, so the fans sold very quickly and in large numbers. Ikkyu spent the entire day signing and selling stacks of Chinese fans.

In the evening, he brought a sack of money to the parents of his prospective "bride." He said, "Look at this! Will this be enough to cover your debts?"

"More than enough," the couple exclaimed excitedly.

With that, Master Ikkyu turned and left their home to go back to his monastery.

Stories About

PEOPLE

A NEIGHBOR'S LOVE

Chang Shao-ying was a lively and happy child who could be heard laughing and running around all day long. The kids in her neighborhood used to love to play with her. Then one day when she was five years old, Shao-ying became very ill with a disease that caused a severe weakening of her legs. She became unable to walk and was forced to leave school and stay home for a long time. The change was hard on her. Whereas before she had been able to go to school and play with her friends all day long, now she was stuck in the house wearing a pair of braces on her legs, trying to learn how to walk again. She responded to her new conditions by becoming angry at herself and gloomy toward the world.

She threw her toys around the house, cried often, and frequently quarreled with her parents. No matter what Mrs. Chang tried to do, she was not able to control her daughter. Before long, she had no choice but to let Shao-ying to do whatever she wanted.

One day, the Changs' neighbor across the street, Mrs. Wang, was rushing out the door with her briefcase under her arm to go to work when she heard Shao-ying crying. Mrs. Wang, who was a practicing Buddhist, felt sorry for the little girl, so she went into the house to try to comfort her.

"Go away! I don't need your help!" Shao-ying yelled at her, before hobbling toward another room to get away from Mrs. Wang.

Though her words had been very sharp, Mrs. Wang was not upset by the little girl's rudeness. She knew that she had not been able to control herself. From that day on, she began to stop at the Changs' quite frequently to spend time with Shao-ying. At first the little girl was suspicious, but as time went by, she became more used to Mrs. Wang. Mrs. Wang always spoke with great kindness to Shao-ying, and she encouraged her in every way she could. Before long, Shao-ying began to act like her old self again, and the Changs' house was filled once more with laughter and joy. Seven years went by, and during that time Mrs. Wang and Shao-ying became like mother and daughter to each other.

Then, suddenly, Mrs. Wang had to move away. Shao-ying cried for days. When her tears finally stopped, however, she was even gentler and more considerate than she had been before. After school she willingly helped around the house, and she did everything she could to share her parents' hardships and problems. She became a wonderful daughter, and everything in the house went smoothly and easily because of her.

Once, not long after that, Mrs. Chang told one of her friends, "I am so grateful to Mrs. Wang, I don't know what to say. I gave birth to my daughter, but it was Mrs. Wang who gave all of us the gift of life."

A FATHER'S REGRETS, A MOTHER'S LOVE

Kuei Hua had bad fate. When her children were still very young, her husband ran off with another woman and never contacted her again.

Kuei Hua had no choice but to hire herself out as a maid, and raise her children alone. Fortunately, her three children were capable and bright. Some fifteen years later, one of them was in a Ph.D. program, one was in college, and one was in high school.

Coincidentally, at the end of one year, all three of Kuei Hua's children were scheduled to graduate from their respective schools, and all of them were due to receive honors awards.

To celebrate their "triple happiness," Kuei Hua, who had been a Buddhist for years, made a wonderful vegetarian meal that all four of them could enjoy at home in peace as they reflected on the good things that life had brought them.

Just as everyone's spirits were rising with the occasion, Kuei Hua suddenly lowered her head and sighed. "Oh," she said, "if only your father could see all of you now. He would be so proud of you!"

In the space of a moment, Kuei Hua's words had totally ruined the atmosphere in the room. Her oldest son said, "Mom! Don't talk about that now! It was he who chose to abandon us. We don't need to feel sorry for him, or care about him at all!"

Her daughter added, "That's right! He's the one who ran off with another woman. He didn't care about what happened to us. He left everything up to you! Why would anyone want to mention his name now?"

"Listen," Kuei Hua said. "No matter what happened, he is still your father. You must not remain resentful for your whole life."

Just then, there was the noise outside of someone moving and then running away. Kuei Hua opened the door and looked out. In the semi-dark, she saw the bedraggled form of a beggar in a torn shirt scooting down the street. Something in the posture and movement of the beggar's form reminded her of something. She called to her children, "Quick! Don't let him get away!"

Kuei Hua's children raced out the door and quickly caught up with the beggar. The three of them escorted him back to their mother's kitchen and sat him down in the light. His face was drawn and forlorn. Without further ceremony, he began to speak.

"That woman took all my money and ran off just a few weeks after I left to go live with her. I had nowhere to go, and then I started wandering, and then I became sick, and then I was just too ashamed to come back. Recently, I heard that all you kids were graduating with honors. I couldn't help myself. I just had to come back and take a look in the window.

"I saw you all sitting there and when I heard what you were saying about me, I felt so bad I just could not stand it anymore. I had to run away. I feel so sorry for what I did!"

"One moment of honest repentance will absolve the sins of three lifetimes," Kuei Hua said. "Your fifteen years is nothing compared to that. If you really are sorry for what you did, you can be forgiven."

As she spoke, a wonderful expression of wisdom, benevolence, and

compassion formed on her face. Then Kuei Hua began to smile. She smiled
at her children and then she smiled quietly at her children's father.

And he never left her house again.

THE WILD CRANE IS FREE TO SOAR

Chung Nan-p'ing was a powerful figure in the
world of business. She became the general manager of her company when
she was only thirty years old. The directors of her company treated her
with great deference and respect, while those who were below her carried
out her smallest wishes almost before she expressed them. She was often
praised by her company's clients for her efficiency and intelligence, and
others in her field, who best understood what she was doing, admired her
for the way she conducted herself.

What no one understood, however, was that beneath her capable and
efficient exterior, Chung harbored many fears and self-doubts. This pro-
duced an enormous inner strain on her since, day after day, she had to
maintain the image of herself that she had created for the world. She had to
deal with all kinds of people and handle all sorts of difficult situations.
Eventually, the pressures generated by these contradictions caused her to
develop ulcers. For a while, she continued on in her old ways, but as her
health deteriorated and she lost more weight, she began to feel that her life
was empty and without meaning.

She began to ask herself, "What is life really all about? What does it
really mean?"

Then a friend convinced her to go on a Buddhist retreat, where for nine
days she was required to think and act like a nun. The retreat helped Chung
see her life in a new light. She began to regret the pride and vanity that had
characterized the world she had been living in. Instead of being praise-
worthy, she began to understand that the conceits of that world were
defilements which had only served to block her vision of the truth. After
the retreat was over, Chung's first act on returning to the "dust" of this
mundane world was to resign from her job and move back to the small

town of P'ingtung, where she had been raised. Her friends and colleagues all thought Chung had gone a little mad, so one by one they traveled south to see what had happened to her.

What they found was a woman completely changed from her former self. Her hair was cut short and her clothing was simple. The attitude of self-importance that had characterized her in the past had given way to a charming and childlike demeanor. While before Chung had spent her time immersed in the complexities of the corporate world, now she passed her days pruning and weeding in her garden. She did manual labor in all kinds of weather. Without makeup and with her hands soiled, she projected an aura of happiness and well-being that was so genuine it was more impressive by far than anything her former station had boasted to the world.

At first, most people believed her sudden conversion would be short-lived, but as time went by, they came to understand that Chung had changed for good.

Once Chung explained herself to one of her friends. She said, "A caged bird always has food and comfort nearby, but a wild crane is free to soar through the skies. My spirit had been trapped, and when I understood that, I set it free."

A LITTLE GIRL ON A BUS

Right in the middle of summer, when all of Taiwan was hot and humid, a bus full of people slowly wound its way through the streets as everyone on board began nodding off to sleep. Suddenly, a bell rang. "Riiing!" The sound split the silence on the bus. The driver pulled the bus over and opened the doors, but no one got up to leave.

The bus driver closed the doors again and started down the road as before. The bus went through an intersection under a green light, and then "Riiing!"—the bell sounded again. The driver pulled his bus to the side of the road again, but again no one rose to leave. The driver only smiled as he steered the large vehicle back into traffic.

After a while, the bell sounded again. This time a woman spoke up, loudly complaining at her daughter who was sitting in front of her. "Would you stop that, please?" she said. "We all can see what you are doing."

The girl turned and looked sheepishly at her mother as slowly she withdrew her arm from the cable that rang the bell. After that, the bell never sounded again. A few stops later, the mother and daughter got off the bus.

After they had left, a passenger who was sitting just behind the bus driver asked, "How can you possibly be so patient? You didn't seem to have been irritated in the least by that."

"The truly patient one is him," the driver said as he pointed to a figure of Buddha fixed to his dashboard. "I am simply trying to learn from him."

THERE ARE EYES IN HEAVEN

Dr. Liu Ch'ang-ming was a devout Buddhist.
One year he was invited to attend a medical conference in London.

On the day he was scheduled to leave for the conference, some of Dr. Liu's friends went to the airport to send him off. When Dr. Liu did not arrive to catch his plane for England, his friends became worried about him and called around to see what had happened. At last they got through to him at the hospital.

Dr. Liu had been on his way to the airport when he had witnessed an automobile accident in which a young woman had been seriously injured. Dr. Liu had stopped to help. He had provided emergency care for the young woman right at the scene, and then he had taken her to the hospital himself to finish treating her injuries.

Naturally, Dr. Liu was unable to catch his flight to London that day. By the time he finally did get to his conference in England, he discovered that he had already missed more than half of it. On the plane back to Taiwan from England, he was more than a little disappointed that he had traveled all that way only to miss most of what had happened at the conference.

Dr. Liu's son met him at the airport in Taiwan. With him was a young woman who also seemed very happy to see Dr. Liu.

"Dad! You saved us! Now we can get married!" his son said, beaming with gratitude and affection.

"What?" Dr. Liu said.

It turned out that the young woman he had saved a few days earlier was none other than his son's girlfriend. His son had been trying to marry her for two years, but all his requests had been flatly refused by his girlfriend's father because her father had a strong antipathy for doctors. The father disliked doctors because his wife had died due to a mistake made by a doctor some years before. Accordingly, he refused to allow his daughter to marry into a medical family.

When the man learned, however, that his daughter's life had been saved by a doctor who was the father of her boyfriend, he decided that he no longer could refuse to give his daughter away in marriage.

When Dr. Liu heard this story, he was so overcome with joy that he could hardly contain himself. He clapped his hands and gazed toward the sky. Then he said, "Amitabha! At the time of the accident, I was only thinking of saving this young woman's life. I never could have imagined that I was also saving the life of my own daughter-in-law! Amitabha! Amitabha! Truly, there are eyes in Heaven!"

A SUCCESSFUL BENEFACTOR

Hsu Liang-wang worked for the post office in T'aoyuan, Taiwan. One day, he became head of the Buddha's Light International Association chapter for postal workers. Hsu was very good at his work and helpful with everyone. He was so good at working with people, in fact, that his friends encouraged him to run for political office. Whenever they pressed him to enter the elections, however, Hsu would only smile and say nothing in reply

Then one day, he donated one million yuan to the Buddha's Light University Foundation fund. When his friends heard about that, they asked him, "Why didn't you use that money to run for a seat in the legislature? Why did you just throw it away on a donation to the university?"

Hsu answered, "If I used that money to run for office, I might spend it all and still not get elected. By giving it to Buddha's Light University, however, I became a successful benefactor at once!"

A LATE GUEST

Darkness had fallen. Stars flickered in the sky.
Evening chanting services had already ended. The incense master had thrown the bolt across the great door of Buddha Hall.

He walked a few steps away from the large doors when he saw an old woman running up the stairs toward him. She was gasping with exertion when she spoke, "Master! Master! Wait a moment! I want to make a donation."

"The hall is closed for the night. I'm sorry. Can you come again tomorrow?"

As the incense master was speaking, the abbot of the temple, Hsin Ting, drew near enough to hear the old woman's reply.

"I'm sorry," she said, "but I've come all the way from Hualien. It took me all day to get here. I couldn't help but be late. Today is the day I promised Buddha I would make a donation to the temple. I've been selling old newspapers for a year to save money to make this donation. Please let me go inside! I promised I would make the donation today!"

When Hsin Ting heard what the woman had to say, he stepped forward to greet her. Then he asked the incense master to open Buddha Hall so she could go inside. Hsin Ting then waited quietly until she was finished. When the old woman came out again, the monk personally escorted her to Pilgrimage Hall where he helped her register for the night.

The next morning, when it was time for the old woman to leave, she stood for a long time gazing at a golden statue of Buddha as tears slowly ran from her eyes. A nun standing beside her heard her say, "In my whole life I have never been treated this well by anyone."

SPIRITUAL WEAPONRY

General Yeh Ching-jung was commander of the
Republic of China's forces on Chinmen Island, which lies just off the coast of mainland China.

General Yeh often invited monastics from Buddha's Light Mountain to go to Chinmen to speak about Buddhism to his troops, and while they were there, he always treated them with great respect. When I went there on one occasion myself, General Yeh went so far as to order all his officers to come hear me preach the Dharma.

After a while, some people began to question what General Yeh was doing. They asked, "Is it a good idea to teach the army Buddhism? How can Buddhism possibly make them stronger and more courageous?"

Someone even reported General Yeh to the Ministry of Defense. In the report they said, "If you spend time teaching your troops compassion, patience, meditation, and generosity, do you really think they will be able to fight when war comes?"

Even some of our monastics began to worry that General Yeh might get in trouble if we kept preaching the Dharma to his soldiers. They said to him, "We can keep preaching the Dharma if you want, but maybe it would be better for you if we did not."

General Yeh replied, "In the past, the military only thought of military defenses, never of spiritual defenses, and our government just thought of control and power, never of compassion and real justice.

"I'm not inviting you to come here because I am a Buddhist and therefore want everyone else to be a Buddhist. I am inviting you to come here because I have thought deeply about these matters, and I believe that Buddhism can teach us how to arm ourselves, not just with guns, but also with a sort of spiritual weaponry. Buddhism can teach us patience, it can teach us compassion, and it can teach us to think clearly. Buddhism can only be a good influence on the army because the most important part of an army is not the guns, but the minds of the men."

FRUIT FACES

Late one afternoon, Mrs. Ch'iu prepared a bowl of fruit for her family and set it on the table. When her son came home from school, he saw the fruit and began drawing faces on it.

When Mrs. Ch'iu came into the room again, she saw that all of the fruit that she had prepared had faces drawn on it. In the rush of the moment, she lost control of herself and picked up a rattan stick to strike her son. In response the boy raised himself up, and with great confidence said to his mother, "Mom! I didn't do anything wrong! Why are you going to hit me?"

"Look at what you've done," his mother said. "You've drawn faces on all of the fruit!"

"Mom! I did that for a reason. Grandma likes to eat bananas so I drew her face on the bananas so no one else would take them. Sister likes apples, so I drew her face on the apples so brother wouldn't take them."

As soon as Mrs. Ch'iu learned why her son had drawn faces on the fruit, she felt ashamed for becoming angry so quickly. She hugged her son as a way of apologizing to him, and said, "Aren't you wonderful! Here I was blaming you when all along it was me who was wrong!"

A CHILD'S LOVE

Mrs. Li was addicted to gambling. Every day of the week she went to a friend's house to play mahjong. It was normal for her to give her children money for food and then stay away all day long gambling until eleven o'clock at night.

Mrs. Li had four children. Among them, her son Hsiao Kuo was the most sensitive and considerate. Every day Hsiao Kuo saved his lunch money. When he returned home after school, he cleaned the house and made sure everything was in good order. At night, he made dinner for the rest of the family, and when eleven o'clock came around, he would always go out to meet his mother and walk her home.

If his mother looked downcast, Hsiao Kuo would know that she had lost for the day. Despite her gambling, Hsiao Kuo thought highly of his mother. It was difficult for him to resolve the reality of her having lost all her money with his image of her as a powerful and capable person. For this reason, Hsiao Kuo developed the habit of giving his mother whatever money he had managed to save during the week if he saw she had lost during the day. He usually would pass her the money in the shadows of an alley as they walked home together. If his mother asked him where the money had come from, Hsiao Kuo always said, "Dad gave it to me to give to you."

Whenever her son said that, Mrs. Li felt warmly comforted by the care and concern she thought that she was receiving from her husband and family.

When she arrived home, her other children would be waiting quietly. In their eyes, she was a very impressive woman because every day she seemed to be able to win at the mahjong table and bring snacks back home for them to eat.

Mr. Li, who worked a regular job all week long, was a quiet and honest person. Even though he was bothered by the fact that his wife was spending all her time gambling, still, he reasoned, the children were happy and their home was quiet, so there was no point disturbing everyone by saying anything to his wife about what she was doing.

The people in the Li's small town thought that they were a model couple. Everyone knew the Lis never fought, and from the outside it seemed that everything was fine at home. Whenever someone complimented Mrs. Li on her marriage, she would reply, "I am lucky. I married a good man."

One day, Hsiao Kuo's teacher came for a routine visit to the Lis' home. While he was there, he informed Mrs. Li that her son always hid in a corner of the playground at lunch time and that he rarely had more than a piece of bread or two for his meal.

The moment he told her that, Mrs. Li understood what had really been happening in her home, and how much strain she had been causing her family by her constant gambling. She began to cry, and decided in that instant to quit mahjong for good.

"My little Hsiao Kuo is too good for me," she said through her tears.

PRACTICE WHAT YOU PREACH

One day an old man named Shen died of heart failure during a trip he was taking to Australia. Shen was from Taiwan, and when Ch'en Yu-te of the Australian Buddha's Light International Association learned that there was no one to care for the body, he stepped forward to help. Ch'en reasoned that both he and Shen had been born in the same country, and therefore, he owed it to Shen to do his best to help him as much as he could.

Ch'en bought a coffin for Shen and then gathered members of the Buddha's Light International Association to chant sutras for him. Ch'en worked hard to contact Shen's relatives in Taiwan, but all he found was a daughter who had been put up for adoption when she was very young. Her economic circumstances were not good, and she barely was able to afford the trip to Australia for her father's funeral. Ch'en was aware that it would be too much for her to pay the costs of having her father's body shipped back to Taiwan, where it could be laid to rest under the ground on which it had lived.

Out of compassion for the daughter and respect for the man, Ch'en promised to undertake all of Shen's final expenses himself, including the cost of sending the body back to Taiwan. Ch'en was not wealthy either, but made a deal with the funeral parlor that he would work for them for a few months to pay off Shen's bill. At the same time, Ch'en talked an airline company into shipping Shen's body back to Taiwan for a lower price than they usually charged. Due to Ch'en's considerable efforts, Shen's body, which had come to an end on foreign soil, was returned at last to his native land. Everything went well for Shen, but due to his deal with the funeral parlor, Ch'en himself subsequently lost his regular job.

Some of his friends asked him, "You were not related to Shen. Why did you feel it was so necessary to go to all that trouble for him?"

Ch'en replied, "My religious beliefs tell me that a person can do without everything in the world, but he can never do without compassion. From what has happened, I have increased my understanding of the significance of life. Already, I feel that I have been rewarded for doing what I believed was right."

Within another month, Ch'en had found a new job that was even better than the one he had lost.

WHERE IS YOUR BUDDHA NATURE?

At fourteen, Lu Hai-hsiang already was pretty tough.
He was a small, wiry kid, but he had strong ideas and a strong tendency to want to go his own way. School was like prison to him. His home life was full of problems. He didn't like most people, and he didn't trust anyone who was older than he was. The only time he felt happy was when he was hanging around with his gang of friends who all had pretty much the same attitude toward life as he did. Only when they were all together, standing loosely on the edge of school grounds, was Lu able to have some sense that he actually belonged in this world.

One day, inevitably, his gang of friends got in a fight with another gang of friends. The police caught most of the boys and took them to the police station. After recording the boys' names and taking their fingerprints, the police told them to call home to have a parent or guardian come down to pick them up.

With those instructions, Lu felt really stunned for the first time that day. He thought, "Who am I going to call? I never know where my mother is and my father has long since gone gambling and drinking."

Lu stood alone for a long time trying to think of what to do. Finally, he decided to call one of his teachers at school. If he didn't call anybody, he knew he would have to spend even more time in the police station.

When his teacher showed up, he said very little to Lu. He took care of the formalities required by the police and left the station building with Lu beside him. The two strolled down the street in silence. It was a silence Lu has remembered all his life because it stood in such sharp contrast to the bright and colorful lights of the busy city around them.

At Lu's front door, his teacher handed him a warm take-out meal he had purchased for him. Then he said, "You know, I believe everybody has a Buddha nature inside. Each one of us can become a Buddha and do great things. All we have to do is discover where our Buddha nature is."

Those words hit home, and thirty years later, long after Lu had grown up and changed his ways, he still remembered them.

After he became a successful businessman, Lu gave much of his time to helping young people. Whenever he was with them, and especially when he found himself with a group of tough young boys, Lu often would ask them in a voice thick with meaning, "Do you know where your Buddha nature is?"

DEVOTEES

BEHIND THE SCENES

When Buddha's Light Mountain was first being built, a young woman came to visit. She was about twenty years old. When she saw the work we were doing on the mountain, she decided then and there to stay and help in Kuole Restaurant, where we generated some of the funds used to support Great Compassion Nursery School.

She was a cheerful person. Whenever I passed the restaurant, I would see her smiling. If there were only a few customers inside, I would see her cheerfully straightening tables or doing the other small tasks required of her. If the restaurant was very busy and packed with people, she would be calm and helpful as she made sure that each diner was well taken care of. From morning to night, day after day, she persisted in doing difficult menial labor with an attitude of willingness and kindness all of us would do well to emulate.

I have watched her for over thirty years, as her dark black hair has slowly turned to grey. Out of respect and admiration for her contributions to Buddhism, we have provided her with living quarters at Buddha's Light Mountain. Her name is Kuo Tao-kuang.

Great Compassion Nursery School frequently wins prizes for excellence and we often are complimented on the good work we do. Whenever people speak to me about how good the school is, I can never help but think of people like Kuo Tao-kuang, who selflessly and tirelessly worked for years only to benefit others. And I wonder, How many of us are really sufficiently appreciative of all the people in the world like her who have contributed so much to our continuing growth and development? Where would any of us be without them?

HELLO TEACHER!

"Hello, teacher!"

When Ts'ai Hung-ts'ai heard those words directed at her for the first time, she was deeply moved.

Ts'ai, who had only graduated from elementary school, was a more or less "ordinary" Taiwanese housewife. Her days were spent fully engaged in the concerns of shopping, cooking, raising her children, and caring for her husband. The world outside her home was interesting but, Ts'ai felt, quite remote from her own much more pressing and practical one. Besides, with the little education she had received, Ts'ai believed it was not her place to ask for too much from the world beyond her home.

Then Ts'ai joined Buddha's Light International Association, and her whole world opened up. She learned to care not only for her husband and her children, but she also came to understand that all people in the world were intimately related to one another and that all people were worthy of her concern.

One year, when Ts'ai heard about the World Buddhist Examination, she became very enthusiastic and volunteered to help. The test was to be given to all age groups as a way of encouraging people to study Buddhism. Ts'ai worked very hard going door to door to register people for the examination. She paid particular attention to elementary school children.

Many people were impressed by her dedication, so when it came time to give the exam, Ts'ai was delegated to go to an elementary school to administer it. The people who met her at the school were all very polite and kind to her, but what impressed Ts'ai the most was the little children. The moment she entered her classroom, all forty of them stood up at once from their desks, bowed deeply and said in unison, "Hello, Teacher!"

After the bell rang and the exam started, all the young students became very quiet and still as they concentrated on their tests. The only person in the room whose heart was still swirling was Ts'ai because never in her life had she ever imagined anyone would ever call her "Teacher." She had merely graduated from elementary school!

When the exam was over and their papers were all packed away, many of the little examinees came up to Ts'ai to say good-bye to her. "Teacher," they asked, "are you coming back tomorrow?"

"See you later, Teacher!"

"Good-bye, Teacher!"

When Ts'ai told me this story, her eyes reddened as she spoke. Then they filled with tears. "That was such a wonderful experience," she said. "I am so grateful to Buddhism for everything it has given me. How else could I ever have known those feelings in this life?"

FEARLESSNESS

Ch'en Yu-ming was the second son of Ch'en Lu-an, a former leader of the Republic of China's Executive Yuan. Yu-ming received a Ph.D. from Harvard University and returned to Taiwan, where he continued studying for another year at Buddha's Light Mountain's Pei Hai Buddhist College.

In 1995, Yu-ming had an opportunity to visit South Africa. While he was there, something happened which showed him that there was even more value to learning Buddhism than he had yet realized.

One evening, he decided to take a walk on the beach. Yu-ming was all alone when suddenly four young men appeared in front of him. One of them brandished a knife and demanded that Yu-ming give them all his money. Yu-ming answered, "If you really have a need, I will be more than willing to help you in any way I can. However, right now I don't have any money on me. I just came out to take a walk along the beach. I am sorry."

Yu-ming was so polite and sincere in his manner, the young men who tried to rob him were quite moved. The five of them began talking together, and before long they all felt like old friends.

When Yu-ming returned to Taiwan, he told his family about what had happened to him. After he finished his story, his father asked him, "Were you afraid?"

"I was not afraid at all," Yu-ming replied.

"Were you angry with them?"

WHERE IS YOUR BUDDHA NATURE?

"I was not angry with them at all. I honestly wanted to help them."

"Now that it's all over, what do you feel?" his father posed this one last question to him.

"This is the first time I have truly understood the direct practical value of always being kind to others."

LOTUS GESTURE

One summer while Ch'en Chun-yi was on a trip, he had a short layover in Thailand. While he was waiting in the airport, Ch'en's wallet was stolen by a pickpocket. His passport and airline ticket were still safe in another pocket, but all of his money had disappeared with the thief.

Ch'en became nervous when he realized that he had no way to pay his airport tax, or to take care of other necessities that might suddenly arise. Then he had a moment of inspiration: Ch'en remembered that he was a member of the Buddha's Light International Association (BLIA) and that the BLIA was an international organization. Wouldn't there be a good chance that some member of the BLIA would pass through the airport in the next hour or so?

Ch'en thought there would be, so he decided to stand in front of the main doors of the airport, where he could greet everyone who came in with the lotus gesture of the BLIA. His idea worked rather quickly. After only a few minutes, a member of BLIA who was in Thailand on a business trip noticed Ch'en and came over to him.

The two of them were happy to meet each other, and when the man learned what Ch'en's problem was, he was even happier to extend the hand of friendship by lending Ch'en enough money to pay his airport tax and meet any unexpected needs.

From that point on Ch'en's return flight to Taiwan was a breeze. Today, Ch'en still enjoys telling the story of the lotus gesture and the pleasure of finding a helping hand just when he needed one most.

54

THE WHOLE WORLD IS YOURS

When a huge fire swept through Mrs. Yang's home, she barely managed to escape with her life. Outside, as she watched the flames and looked around for her family, she was startled, and then terrified, to hear the cries of her little daughter, who had been trapped in a room downstairs. Without another thought, Mrs. Yang ran back into the burning building to save the girl.

She managed to carry her child to safety, but the smoke and the flames had injured her so seriously that she died in the hospital only a few hours later.

Mrs. Yang wept for days. During that time, she was frequently harrowed by the frail sound of her daughter crying for help. Mrs. Yang had no belief in Buddhism, but in order to do every last thing she could think of for her daughter, she went to Buddha's Light Mountain's Taipei Vihara to request that funeral services be held for her child.

"Man's will is not Heaven's will," however. The Taipei Vihara was extremely busy at that time, and not a single monastic could be found to conduct services for Mrs. Yang's daughter. Mrs. Yang was beside herself when she received this news, but as she thought more about what to do, she remembered that a friend of hers had once told her that the editor of Universal Gate magazine was a nun in the Buddha's Light Mountain order. Emboldened by her sense of desperation, Mrs. Yang called the magazine and asked to speak to Venerable Yung Yun, the editor.

She said, "My poor daughter is still at the mortuary, and she can't wait any longer. She is scheduled to be cremated very soon."

When Yung Yun heard this, she agreed to come right over and chant the *Amitabha Sutra* for her. Though matters finally went more or less the way she wanted them to, Mrs. Yang discovered that there was no comfort to be derived from the lonely peace that followed her daughter's inurnment. She cried often, and when she stopped, she fell into the deeper silence of remorse and despair.

One day, when she thought her pain could get no worse, she suddenly remembered something Venerable Yung Yun had said to her after her daughter's funeral. "Love is not something that should be confined to one's own child," the nun had said. "Love can be given to many people, and it should be given to many people. At Taipei Vihara we have art classes for children, and a nursery school for children. Come by some time. We could use your help."

Mrs. Yang decided to do as Yung Yun had advised. Within a year of that day, she became one of Taipei Vihara's most active counselors for young people. Her days were passed usefully and happily since at last she had managed to transform her own suffering into a positive gift she could share with others.

One day she said to Yung Yun, "I lost my daughter, and she can never be replaced, but because of your words, I have gained a whole world."

THIS IS MY HOME

During the Sino-Japanese War, T'ai Pao-ch'eng was made deaf in both his ears. After coming to Taiwan, he helped out at Shou Shan Temple. Later, when Buddha's Light Mountain was established, T'ai became a cook in the restaurant located in Pilgrimage Hall. He worked there peacefully and quietly for twenty years.

Since he could hear nothing at all, T'ai was forced to pay extra attention to the small details of the kitchen. One of the hardest jobs in the kitchen was to determine how much food needed to be made each day. It was always difficult to predict how many people would arrive, or how many might suddenly leave the mountain. With his sharp eye for the world around him and his attentiveness to detail, T'ai became very good at estimating how much rice to make and how many vegetables to prepare. He was never moody and never involved in any sort of conflict with anyone. Even if he were not feeling well, he still would show up for work and do his job to the best of his ability.

After travel between Taiwan and mainland China was permitted again in 1987, his supervisor thought it would only be right to offer to pay T'ai's travel expenses back to his home for a visit. When he told T'ai what he had decided, T'ai replied simply, "Go back to what home? This is my home. I have nowhere else to go."

T'ai's supervisor accepted his refusal, but upon hearing what his reasons were, he immediately arranged for T'ai to be given lodgings at Buddha's Light Mountain for the rest of his life.

ONE OF BUDDHA'S WORKERS

Ts'eng Liang-yuan was the general manager of Tungyu Construction Company. When he became aware of how difficult it was for Buddha's Light Mountain to find a place to establish its Taipei temple, he looked around until he found a good building near the Taipei Sungshan train station. He then helped get the necessary permits to put the temple in the building, and he helped with the down payment for the floors of the building we were going to use. His help was invaluable.

In 1994, we opened our temple on the thirteenth and fourteenth floors. The completed Taipei Vihara fulfilled the wishes of thousands of devotees in Taipei, and from the day it opened, the Vihara has always been full of people coming and going.

One day Ts'eng thought to himself, "There are so many monastics working here, there ought to be somebody who understands the ways of the world living near them so they can do their work more smoothly." To fulfill this need, he quit his job and bought an apartment a few floors beneath the Vihara.

From then on, he spent his days helping manage the practical affairs of the Vihara. Ts'eng was capable and well liked by everyone. Pretty soon, the other residents in the building wanted him to become head of the building's tenants association.

Ts'eng refused them with an engaging mixture of pride and humility. "I am a simple lay worker at the Vihara," he said, "and that is all."

Some of the residents pressed him a little further. "It's hard to understand you," they said. "You quit a powerful job to become an ordinary worker for the Vihara. And now, when people want to promote you, you refuse them. Why?"

Ts'eng answered, "Remember, the great Kuan Kung is also a mere "ordinary worker" for Buddhism. There is nothing better than working at a temple, and there is nothing that can raise me above this. The rewards one gains here surpass anything one can gain anywhere else."

LOYALTY

Wu T'ien-tz'u worked for a printing company in Ilan. Every day after work, he would come to Lei Yin Temple to pray. In time, his faith increased to the point that he decided he wanted to give his life in service to Buddhism by entering the monastery as a monk. Wu's only doubt lay in himself: he wondered if he were good enough and wise enough to offer himself as a monk.

At that time, very few men in Taiwan were becoming monks, so when Wu's friend, Hsiao Pi-hsia, heard what he wanted to do, she was very supportive. She said, "If you decide to become a monk, I promise I will support you in every way I can. I will stand by you for the rest of my life."

Hsiao's encouragement was exactly what Wu needed to hear. He put his doubts behind him, left his job at the printing company, shaved his head, and became Venerable Hsin P'ing.

Hsin P'ing was a very capable monk. Before long, he became the abbot of Lei Yin Temple. During the time that he presided over the temple, his old friend Hsiao was always nearby. She upheld her promise to him in every way that she could. She made herself a dependable presence who could be called on for work or conversation whenever Hsin P'ing needed her. She did menial work, office chores, and any other task that was needed at the temple. Through the years, she continued to encourage Hsin P'ing and give him emotional support whenever she thought it would be helpful.

In 1995, Hsin P'ing was made abbot of Buddha's Light Mountain monastery and temple. His friend Hsiao Pi-hsia followed him up the mountain and continued to provide whatever help she could. She did whatever needed to be done, including cleaning rooms, making beds, and cooking in the kitchen.

When she was still very young, Hsiao had promised Hsin P'ing that she would support him for the rest of her life, and never once did she turn back from that promise. Loyalty like hers is one of the highest functions of the human heart. Without it, nothing of value can ever be built.

INNER ENGINES

Yu Ts'e-lang was a salesman for an engine manufacturer in Chiayi, Taiwan. He was also an active member of the local branch of Buddha's Light International Association. He worked hard for Buddhism all year long, but each year, just before Chinese New Year, he would work even harder. Several days prior to New Year's, Yu would always come with a couple of his friends to help set up the display of "Peace Lanterns" we used to celebrate the occasion.

Coincidentally, the end of the year was also a very good time for selling the kinds of engines Yu sold. People often asked him, "Why do you always go to Buddha's Light Mountain just when business is best? What good can that do you?"

Yu would always answer with great seriousness, "When people come here and see the lanterns and worship Buddha, they feel renewed and are willing to continue with life in a positive manner. I may not be selling engines in town, but by being here I am restarting the engines in people's hearts."

I've watched Yu come to help for years. He's always smiling and friendly and considerate of others. Yu has not only started the engine in his own heart, he has lighted the brilliant lamp of Buddhism, as well.

BUDDHA'S LIGHT TEA

Ting Su-mei lived in Taichung. Before she became a Buddhist, she had no religious belief whatsoever.

Several years ago, during a very hot period in the middle of the summer, she came to Buddha's Light Mountain as a tourist wanting to see the sights. As she strolled around the mountain top looking at the statues and buildings, she gradually became quite warm. Pretty soon she began to perspire and feel thirsty. As she passed Buddha Hall, she was relieved to be approached by a lay worker who asked if she would like to come inside for a glass of tea.

"Please try a glass of Buddha's Light tea," the young woman said to her.

Ting went inside, and immediately her head was filled with the delightful aroma of steeping tea. Other people in the room were happily passing the time, conversing and enjoying the tea. Ting finished her glass and then took out one hundred yuan to give to the young woman who had asked her to come inside.

When the young woman saw what Ting was doing, she waved her hand in polite refusal.

"We have a rule here," she said by way of explanation. "We don't talk about others, and we don't take money from anyone. We just talk about the Dharma and drink tea."

Ting laughed when she heard that and asked why the monastery would make a rule like that.

"Master Hsing Yun made the rule over ten years ago," the young woman explained. "At the time, he noticed that people who came to our monastery needed a place to rest and enjoy themselves for a while, so he set aside this room for that purpose. Since then, you know, Buddha's Light tea has become pretty famous. People who come here now expect to have Buddha's Light tea. So many people want it, in fact, we have set up several other rooms where you can also get Buddha's Light tea."

"It is good tea," Ting said.

"I'm glad you have enjoyed it, and I hope that you will be like the others and come back for more very soon."

Ting really did enjoy the tea. After that first visit she began returning almost once a month to Buddha's Light Mountain. Whenever she came, she always brought friends or relatives with her, and the first thing she always did was go straight to have some Buddha's Light tea.

Once someone asked her, "What's so great about Buddha's Light tea? Taiwan has many great teas. Why do you think that one is so special?"

"Other teas are good, that's true," Ting said, "but only Buddha's Light tea carries the flavor of the Dharma in it. One sip of that tea can change your whole life."

A PROMISE

After Liao Jui-fu moved to Taipei, he became a regular participant in Universal Gate Temple's Friday night Ch'an meditation sessions. A few years later, he retired and started coming to the temple every day to help in one way or another.

A person who frequently volunteers to work at a Buddhist temple sometimes is called a "Guardian of the Temple." After Liao became a "Guardian of Universal Gate Temple," his friends began to wonder what had happened to him because they rarely saw him anymore. Liao explained to everyone, "I have two homes now: one is my regular home that all of you know, and the other is Universal Gate Temple where I spend almost as much time."

His life went on like that for nine more years until he decided to move to Canada to be with his children. Just before he left Taiwan, Liao arranged to have a retired old soldier come to work in his place at the temple. Liao paid the old soldier a good wage to come every day for a full year to take over his duties.

When the nuns at the temple heard what he had arranged, they told him, "Mr. Liao, we are grateful that you are concerned about the temple, but there is no need to hire someone to come work in your place! Universal Gate Temple has many guardians who will be able to fill in for you. You should relax and enjoy your move to Canada."

When he heard them say that, Liao's face became perfectly still.

"No, I can't do that," he said. "Years ago I vowed that I would work here as a guardian for ten years. There is still one year left. I would never be happy in Canada if I left here without fulfilling my vow."

BELIEVING VERSUS
PRACTICING BUDDHISM

Ts'ao Chung-chih is the founder of Taiwan's Lifeline suicide prevention hotline. His wife is a dedicated Buddhist. She converted to Buddhism over thirty years ago and has been an ardent practitioner of humanistic Buddhism ever since. When she first became a Buddhist, Mrs. Ts'ao often spoke about Buddhism to her husband and often encouraged him to come to the temple to chant sutras or to listen to lectures. Since Mr. Ts'ao did not believe in Buddhism, he found it difficult to deal with his wife's constant exhortations. Even still, out of love for her, he came to the temple with some regularity.

After one service at the temple, Mrs. Ts'ao grabbed her husband's hand and pulled him over to me. She said, "Master, please help my husband increase his faith. Please teach him how to bow to Buddha."

One look at the discomfort coursing across Mr. Ts'ao's face was enough to tell me to be careful with what I said. "He doesn't need to bow to Buddha," I replied. "All he needs to do is practice Buddhism in his daily life."

Mr. Ts'ao was obviously pleased with my reply, and afterwards he often told his friends, "Master Hsing Yun himself said I don't need to bow to Buddha; I only need to practice Buddhism."

In the years since then, Mr. Ts'ao has expended an immense amount of energy in helping others. He established Taiwan's Lifeline, he frequently helps the needy, he started a scholarship fund for poor students, he donated over ten thousand wheelchairs to the disabled, and he has given large sums of money for disaster relief. Beyond all that, he also has committed himself to helping Buddha's Light Mountain, Hsi Lai Temple in Los Angeles, and our temple in Paris.

Whenever someone compliments him on all the work he has done, Mr. Ts'ao always answers, "Chanting the sutras is not as good as listening to them. Listening to the sutras is not as good as explaining them. Explaining the sutras is not as good as practicing what they say. I am just practicing Buddhism, that's all."

ONLY LOVE CAN WIN LOVE

Over thirty years ago, a woman came to the temple.
Her name was Mrs. Shen. The moment she saw me, she burst into tears. Through her sobs, she said, "Master, I don't think I can come to services tonight! I don't want to live any more . . . My husband has found another woman!"

I knew Mrs. Shen well. When she finished speaking, I said, "I know a way to save your marriage, but I doubt that you can do it." When she heard me say that, she stopped crying and asked me to tell her what my method was. At first I refused, but she pleaded with me. At last I said, "The reason your husband has found another woman is the wife he has argues with him all the time. First, she's resentful about this, then she's angry about that. He has nowhere else to look for happiness except outside his home. You drive him away from you, and then when he goes, you do nothing to bring him back. Instead, you only criticize him and make things even worse. You've made your husband feel as if his own home were a kind of hell."

"What can I do?" she asked, as she started sobbing all over again.

"You have to make a real effort to be good to your husband," I said. "How can you ever expect to win his love through anger and criticism? Only love can win love."

About a half year after that, Mr. Shen, who had never shown any interest in Buddhism, showed up at the temple one day. He wanted to thank me for saving his marriage, and he wanted to donate a piece of land to the temple as a kind of repayment. Apparently, Mrs. Shen had gone home and done what I had told her to do. She started being as pleasant and kind as she knew how to be. Even when she knew her husband was on his way out to see his girlfriend, she remained calm and showed him as much love as she could. Before long, Mr. Shen concluded that his own home was the better place to be and he returned completely to his wife.

Then one day, he became curious and asked her why she had changed so much. She answered, "Because Master Hsing Yun told me, 'Only love can win love.'"

I COULDN'T WAIT ANY LONGER

When T'ien Hsia Publishing Company first brought up the idea of writing my biography, I was not in favor of it. My life's work is to preach the Dharma, not to talk about myself. Since I was friends with the publisher, however, it was hard for me to refuse. In the end, I had no choice but to let my old friend, Kao Hsi-chun, do the book.

Kao chose a young woman named Fu Chih-ying to write it. I remember the first time I spoke with her; she told me rather solemnly, "I am not a Buddhist and I do not believe in Buddhism. For the next couple of years, I will often be by your side, watching you and taking notes. It would be best if you ignored me at those times. I will just be doing my job."

I felt somewhat pressured by the way she acted and the way she spoke to me, but since I had already agreed to the project, I decided that I would just have to put up with it. For a long time, I would have to expose myself to the scrutiny and judgment of someone else.

Two years later, at Hsi Lai Temple in Los Angeles, during a ceremony for taking refuge in Buddhism, I was surprised to see Fu among the people who were becoming Buddhists. After the ceremony, I went up to her and asked why she had decided to become one of us. She said simply, "Because I couldn't wait any longer!"

In the beginning, before she had written *Handing Down the Light* (her biography of Master Hsing Yun), she had seemed to me to be a rather cold person. Now, she seems to exemplify Buddhist wisdom.

EARNING JOY

Years ago, when we were building Shou Shan Temple, one of the laborers was a man named Hsiao Ting-hsun. Though Hsiao had had no special training, I noticed that he was very talented when it came to construction. Some years later when we were ready to begin building Buddha's Light Mountain, I thought of Hsiao and asked him to come and oversee the project.

I remember those early days very well. We did our work without blueprints. We measured things off with a tape measure, and used sticks to draw our plans in the dirt. As we drew, we discussed how we wanted the buildings to look. The two of us talking together in the shade of a tree was pretty much the way the whole of Buddha's Light Mountain was designed. We were often short of money in those days, but I always did my best to be sure Hsiao had enough to pay his workers, and I often asked him if he needed more.

Over the years, communication between the two of us became so good that we hardly needed to talk anymore. I knew what he needed to get the job done, and he knew what I wanted almost before I spoke.

Thirty years passed quickly. Hsiao's children, and eventually even his grandchildren, came to Buddha's Light Mountain to help with construction. Hsiao sometimes would say quite proudly to people, "I'm the guy who built Buddha's Light Mountain."

Over the years, many construction companies tried to take Hsiao away from us. They offered him very high wages, but he always refused to work for anyone else. When people asked him why he had given his life to a cause that paid him so little, he would answer, "I work here not to earn money, but to earn joy. There is no material pleasure in the world that can compare to the joy of doing something valuable."

Stories About

MYSELF

SPEECHLESS CHICKS

One winter when I was seven years old, two of our baby chickens were caught in the rain. When I saw their soaking little bodies, I felt sorry for them. The idea occurred to me to take them into our house and dry their feathers in front of the stove. The chicks didn't know what my plan was so they became afraid. In a moment of commotion they jumped into the stove. By the time I was able to pull them back out of the fire, all of their feathers had been burned off and their little feet were scorched from the coals. Only their tiny beaks had escaped being harmed by the fire. After that I fed them by hand several times a day. As I fed them, I would speak softly to them as a way of comforting them. It took more than a year of this before the chickens were able to fully regain their strength. Eventually they grew into adult birds able to lay eggs. My family and neighbors were surprised that I had been able to nurse them back to health, and they asked me how I had done it. The truth was, all I had done was imagine I was a tiny chicken too, and in that state of mind, I gave them what I thought they needed most.

A CHILD'S HEART

One very cold evening when I was five years old, my family gathered around the stove and began talking and telling stories. My uncle said, "A long time ago there was a poor old man who lived deep in the mountains. He had no family to care for him and every day it was a struggle for him just to get enough to eat and to stay warm. . ." After hearing only that much, I could not control myself and burst into tears.

When my uncle finished his story, my family discovered that I had disappeared. At last they found me under a table still crying so hard my eyes were red and swollen. My mother was concerned about me and said, "What's the matter? Come out of there. You can't stay there crying all night long."

"That poor old man! I feel so sorry for him. We have to do something to help!" I said through my tears.

"That was just a story," my uncle said laughing. "None of that was really true. You don't have to feel sorry for him."

I didn't believe my uncle at all, and I kept crying and pleading with my family to do something for that poor old man. No one could get me to stop, so at last they told me that my grandfather, Liu Wen-tsao, was really the old man in the story, and we all went out in the cold to buy some treats for him. Only then did I stop crying.

A TEACHER'S HEART

At the start of the Sino-Japanese War in 1937, I was ten years old. The year after that, my father went on a short business trip and never returned. We never found out what happened to him. I can still remember accompanying my mother as she went to Nanking in search of news about him. That early and mysterious loss of my father cast a shadow across my heart that was not easily erased.

When I was sixteen, I wrote an essay for school about the feelings I had for my father. The essay was titled "An Undeliverable Letter." My Chinese teacher at that time, Master Sheng P'u, wrote the comment, "Even an iron heart must weep over this." Then he used two whole hours of class time to read my essay to the other students. I felt deeply grateful to him for praising my essay so much. I knew he was expressing love for me by doing that.

About two weeks later, I was startled to learn that "An Undeliverable Letter" had been published in the *New Chiangsu Newspaper*. Master Sheng

P'u came to me one day with a stack of the papers to show me my essay. He told me that he had copied the essay after class and sent it to the paper for submission.

He never said so, but it was clear to me that Master Sheng P'u had not told me about submitting my essay because he had wanted to guard me from disappointment in case it were rejected. I was deeply moved by the sensitivity and compassion he showed in the way he dealt with that essay. I have tried to follow his example all my life in the way I treat others. Since moving to Taiwan, I often have thought of Master Sheng P'u and savored the memory of his kindness.

In 1989, when I went back to mainland China for the first time in forty years, I wanted to thank him in person for what he had done for me, but I was very busy and no chance ever presented itself for me to go see him. All I was able to do was ask someone to visit him for me, and thank him for what he had done so many years before. To this day, I still regret that I was not able to go see him myself.

SNEAKING OUT AT NIGHT

I became an ordained monk when I was fifteen years old. The day before my ordination ceremony was to begin, my mother came to see me. That night, during evening study hours, I went to the nuns' dorm where she was staying to visit her. Before long, the "Great Silence" (a mandatory quiet period after 10:00 P.M.) was called. I was supposed to return to the monks' dorm then, but my mother couldn't bear to let me go. She was crying so hard, her face was covered with tears. I had no choice but to stay with her and comfort her. When the monk who was patrolling the monastery came around to check the nuns' dorm, some of the nuns decided to help me by hiding me in my mother's bed. I spent the night in her room with her.

Early the next morning, just when I was starting to relax for not having been caught the night before, the monk who had patrolled the grounds made his report.

"Last night, Chin Chueh (my monastic name at that time) did not sleep in his bed." He made this report to Master Yueh Chi who was in charge of the ordination ceremony. When I heard him say that to Master Yueh Chi, I became quite nervous. I was afraid I might be punished and have my name removed from the ordination list.

Master Yueh Chi, however, responded gently, "Oh, him. Last night he was with me." When the monk who had patrolled heard that, he was satisfied and went away. You can imagine how grateful I felt toward Master Yueh Chi for his having covered for me.

In 1954, I got a chance to repay Master Yueh Chi for his kindness. When I heard he was in Hong Kong with no friends and no one to help him, I found a way to have him come to Taiwan. Later, I recommended that he be appointed head of a temple in Kaohsiung. When he became old and sick, I often took him to the hospital in the middle of the night for emergency care. I paid all his expenses in his last years and watched over him until his death.

I wonder if he ever guessed exactly why I treated him so respectfully for all those years.

REFUGEES AT
CH'I HSIA SHAN TEMPLE

In 1937, the Sino-Japanese War started. Toward the end of that year, Nanking was taken by the Japanese. In the first days of their occupation, three hundred thousand Chinese were massacred in and around the city.

The weather was cold, the ground was frozen and a powdery snow blew across the land. At that time two monks, Masters Chi Jan and Chih K'ai, were in charge of Ch'i Hsia Shan Temple. (Master Hsing Yun was Master Chih K'ai's disciple.) They decided to turn the temple into a refugee camp, where they would provide whatever aid they could to whomever asked.

Once it was known that food was available at the temple, several hundred thousand refugees began to make their way there. As this huge number of people began pouring in, the monks and workers at the temple were overwhelmed by the enormity of their needs and their suffering. Everybody was cold and many people were starving.

Before long, the temple completely ran out of its normal food stores. Master Chih K'ai said to Master Chi Jan, "In the granary we still have over two thousand pounds of soy beans. The beans are supposed to be used as offerings on the first and the fifteenth of every month; but why don't we use them to make soup for these poor people instead?"

When one of the monks at the temple heard Master Chih K'ai's suggestion, his eyes reddened with annoyance. He said, "We've already given them everything we have. We don't need to give them the last of our soy beans, too!"

Master Chih K'ai responded quite heatedly, "Saving one life is more valuable than saving a whole temple. As Buddhists, we must be willing to sacrifice everything. This is one of those times when we must give up all that we have to help others."

In those terrible times, Ch'i Hsia Shan Monastery became a sort of home and a last resort for hundreds of thousands of people who otherwise would have had nowhere else to go. Master Chih K'ai's passionate plea, which set the tone for the months to come, was like an inextinguishable flame that showed all of us the way out of that terrible darkness.

A HALF BOWL OF PICKLES

I was the only disciple of my master, Chih K'ai, to become an ordained monk. Master Chih K'ai was a very strict teacher. When I was seventeen years old, however, I experienced his compassion and sympathy.

At that time, I became ill with a malarial fever. One moment I was hot, and the next I was cold. My body was in great pain, but I kept to the rules of the time, which dictated that a monk should continue with his ordinary schedule no matter how bad he felt. I continued going to morning and evening chanting services for about two weeks. As the days went by I became very weak and probably was close to dying from the fevers that kept wracking my body. One day, Master Chih K'ai sent someone over to me with a half bowl of pickles.

In those days, we were all so poor, a half bowl of pickles was a real treasure! I knew the pickles Master Chih K'ai had given me were his way of silently showing that he cared about me. Holding back my tears, I ate the whole bowl. And as I ate, I promised myself that I would dedicate the rest of my life to Buddhism as a way of repaying my master for his mercy.

THE SANGHA RELIEF UNIT

In 1949, the Kuomintang and the communists still were fighting fiercely. During the battle of Hsupang, the Kuomintang incurred major losses, while many civilians were driven from their homes. In those terrible circumstances, Master ChihYung decided to establish a Buddhist "Sangha Relief Unit" to help wherever it could. The unit was to be comprised of Buddhist monks. As soon as I learned of Master ChihYung's intention, I volunteered to be part of the unit. The unit was to fall under General Sun Li-jen's command, and it was to contain six hundred Sangha workers.

At the last minute, Master Chih Yung decided not to lead the unit, so I took over. Those were turbulent times, and even as we were still organizing we were told that we would be leaving right away to go to Taiwan with General Sun.

Traveling at night, I made my way through battlefields and across the devastated countryside to get to the T'ien Ning Temple in Ch'ang Chou where other members of the Sangha Relief Unit were staying. I arrived in the dark, and without any ceremony began waking up the people who were supposed to go with us. Vens. Hao Ling, Yin Hai, Ching Hai, and Yi Te were some of the monks I woke up that night. We left the temple without delay and traveled straight to the ship that took us to Taiwan.

Sometimes when I tell this story, people ask me, "Did you know them very well? You must have known those monks well to wake them up like that in the middle of the night."

My answer is: "When the reason is to save lives, I'm not afraid to wake anyone at any time!"

AN UNORTHODOX WAY TO HELP

In 1949, I came to Taiwan because I was part of a relief unit assigned to soldiers who were being sent to the island. Master Hsing Ju was in the same unit with me when we arrived. At the time, he was ill with tuberculosis. He could not get out of bed and his breathing was weak. In those days, tuberculosis was a frightening disease. It killed many people all over the world. Nobody dared to get near him because he was so sick. Those were chaotic times, and there were few material goods available to anyone. It was difficult for me just to find enough to eat. It would have been impossible to pay for a doctor to treat Master Hsing Ju, so I did the best I could for him on my own.

Fortunately, I found an unorthodox way to help him in the back of a book by Master Yin Kuang. Every day I scraped a kind of fuzz off the back of loquat leaves to make a thick soup which I spoon fed him one mouthful at a time. When he showed signs of getting better, I began to give him leeks mixed with rice as well. This caused some problems because people said monks were not supposed to eat leeks. I said, "The man almost died. Why do you care if he eats a few leeks?"

I took care of him like that for half a year, until he had recovered. Later, he moved to Peit'ou to become head of P'u Chi Temple.

UNIVERSAL GATE

Sometimes people ask me, "Why does Buddha's Light Mountain so often use 'Universal Gate' (P'u Men) as a name for its temples and activities?" When I hear them ask that, I can't help but remember how things were when I first came to Taiwan in 1949.

There was a period of time then when I had nowhere to stay and, often, nothing to eat. I remember once going to a temple in those days on Nanch'ang Road in Taipei. An old man at the temple said to me bluntly, "What right did you have to come to Taiwan?" Later that same day, I went to another temple on Chungcheng Road, but I was turned away there, too.

By nightfall, my clothes were soaked from the rain that had been falling all day. I was hungry and I had nowhere to go.

At last I crouched under a large bell and did my best to wait out the night. The next day, I remember peering inside Shan Tao Temple where there was a large group of people sitting around a small table eating lunch. There seemed to be no room at the table for me, so I just watched them for a while, and left.

As I was wandering around after that, it occurred to me to go to Keelung to see a former classmate. I found two friends whose circumstances were no better than mine. The three of us walked all the way from Taipei to Keelung in the cold rain. By the time we finally reached my friend's temple, it was well after one in the afternoon. When my friend there heard that we had had nothing to eat for more than a day, he asked us into the kitchen to give us some food. A monk who was standing nearby said, "Our master has already explained that there is hardly enough food here to feed all of us. You better ask these guys to go somewhere else to look for something to eat." We turned to leave when he said that, but before we could go, my friend insisted on buying us some rice with his own money. He cooked a big pot of rice porridge. I can still remember holding that bowl of warm porridge in my hands. At that point I was so hungry, I was shaking. When we finished eating, we thanked our friend and set out again in the cold rain to wander some more.

Those hard times made a very strong impression on me. I remember vowing to myself at the time that one day the door to my temple would be a "Universal Gate," open to all who wanted to come. No one would be turned away. Twenty years later, I built the Universal Gate Vihara and founded Universal Gate Temple in Taipei.

I ask all my disciples to treat anyone who comes to any of our facilities with the utmost kindness. I want people to feel happy when they visit us, and I want them to want to come back. There is also an unwritten rule among all temples connected with Buddha's Light Mountain: always have extra food at every meal in case someone comes by unexpectedly. And whenever monks from other orders visit us, we always give them five hundred yuan for travel expenses.

So, whenever I start a new school or a magazine, I think of naming it "Universal Gate." I hope everyone one day will learn the spirit of "universalism" and that everyone will practice welcoming other people, instead of turning them away.

GIVING UP MY STUDIES

Chu Tien-yuan works in a bean-paste shop in Kaohsiung, Taiwan. He is a good person and there is no one more helpful in preaching the Dharma.

I remember about thirty years ago, Chu read an article concerning a young woman who had had to sell herself into prostitution to raise money to care for her sick mother. Chu was so moved by the story, he came straight to me to ask if there were any way we could save the young woman from the difficult life she had entered upon. His warmth and caring were more than evident in the concern he showed for her.

In 1957, after I wrote the *Story of Shakyamuni*, I applied to study at Taisho University in Japan. I was accepted into the Buddhist studies program at the university. As I was preparing to go, Chu came to visit me. His expression was dubious and skeptical. "Master," he said, "in our eyes you are our Master and our teacher. To us your standing already is much higher than any Ph.D. I can't understand why you need to go to Japan to be someone else's student."

His words made me think. Originally, I had renounced worldly pleasures to become a monk. My purpose in doing that was to preach Buddhism and help others, and because of that, my life never could be the same as other people's.

We can't live only for ourselves, but each of us must give something to other people, as well. I was Chu's master at that time and he needed me.

I thought, should I really be contemplating going far away to Japan to study academics? How would that make my followers feel? I was a teacher to them, but not a teacher of academics or of worldly matters. What they wanted to learn from me was the transcendental power of Buddhism. They wanted to grow beyond suffering and reach the realization of eternal joy within the Dharma.

The next day, I gave up my plans to go to Japan to study. To this day, I have never regretted that decision. Instead, I think that choice has only helped me to see even deeper into the significance of human life. After listening to Chu, I redirected the energies and desires I had focused on study and put them all into preaching the Dharma. And by doing that, I know I was able to do more for Buddhism and much more for other people.

A HUMANISTIC BUDDHIST

Sun Chang Ch'ing-yang was the wife of General Sun Li-jen. When I was a monk many years ago at Ch'i Hsia Shan Monastery, I often saw her come to pray and listen to the Dharma. I saw her often, but I never once spoke to her.

In 1949, when I first came to Taiwan, there was a rumor that some six hundred communist spies had come to the island disguised as monks. I got caught up in that rumor and was arrested by the Kuomintang, along with many other monks, including Master Tz'u Hang. When Sun Chang Ch'ing-yang heard what had happened to us, she went everywhere she could speaking to people about us and telling them that a mistake had been made. It was due to her efforts that we eventually were released.

When I was thirty, I became editor of *Awakening the World* magazine. On my birthday that year, Sun Chang Ch'ing-yang threw a small party for me. I remember that all of the plates and bowls were made of gold and that Sun Chang treated me with great kindness. On that day she also told me that she wanted to pay for my schooling so I could finish my education. I was quite poor at that time and grateful for her offer, but felt I had to refuse it because my heart lay in preaching the Dharma and not in studying.

Sun Chang contributed a lot to Buddhism. She donated money to Shan Tao Temple. She sold her jewelry to bring the Tripitaka from Japan, and she established the Yi Hua Book Store which helped in publishing many Buddhist texts.

Much of the development of Buddhism in Taiwan today rests on her efforts. Some years ago, due to a political incident involving her husband

(General Sun had a falling out with Chiang Kai-shek in the early 1960s), she retired into her home and rarely went out again. Human feelings can be shallow; after her retirement, she was largely ignored by society. Since I felt so indebted to her for all that she had done for Buddhism, I often went to visit her at her home. When she was near the end of her life, she donated a house in Yung Ho to me, saying she hoped it would become a Buddhist cultural center. Though I knew she had a family to care for her needs after she died, I volunteered to pay for her funeral. Her ashes were placed in the Tomb of Eternal Life at Buddha's Light Mountain.

Plans are now being made to turn the house she donated into the Buddhist center she wanted. It will be a fitting tribute to a real humanistic Buddhist who gave so much of herself to help others.

TO SEE THE SUN AGAIN

In the early 1950s, political and social conditions in Taiwan were highly unsettled and uncertain. The remains of the Kuomintang army had just retreated to Taiwan from mainland China following their loss of the mainland to the Chinese communists. Taiwan was under strict martial law, and fear of invasion or of spies was common.

Ch'en Hsiu-p'ing worked at a power company in the early 1950s. During a routine spot search one day, Ch'en was found with the business card of someone who had been designated a "suspicious bandit" ("bandit" generally meant "communist" in those days) by the authorities. As a result, Ch'en was designated a "suspicious bandit," too. Because of that designation, he was frequently searched and interrogated by Kuomintang officers. Once the stigma of "suspicious bandit" had been affixed to his name, Ch'en found it impossible to free himself from it.

When Ch'en first came to Ilan, no matter where he went or what he did, he was watched by the police. He had little or no freedom of movement. He was frequently harassed and even when he started coming to Buddhist services, the police followed him.

At the time, the Kuomintang government was still not on a firm footing; soldiers were everywhere, and every time the wind blew it seemed the whole country shook. I myself had to be very careful in what I did because monks were also considered to be "suspicious." But as a monk, I had higher responsibilities to think of, too. If any of my disciples were in any kind of trouble, it was my duty and my desire to help them. I felt very disturbed by what was happening to Ch'en Hsiu-p'ing. I told myself I had to do something for him. At last I went to the chief of police in Ilan and told him, "I want to take Ch'en Hsiu-p'ing with me when I go out to preach the Dharma."

"That can not be allowed!" he said. "Ch'en is a 'suspicious bandit.' He must be watched very closely."

I said, "Bandits are people who do bad things to disrupt society and undermine its laws. If I take Ch'en with me to preach the Dharma, he will be helping society. Why won't you allow that? When you prevent him from doing good, it's almost as if you were asking him to do evil."

"Then you have to take full responsibility for everything he does."

"I will take full responsibility for his actions," I said.

From then on, I always took Ch'en with me when I went out to preach the Dharma. He was with me like that for quite a few years. One day, I heard that a business school was being established in Taipei. Following my recommendation, Ch'en was chosen to be vice-chancellor of the school.

A TIRELESS WORKER

Chang Shao-chi became involved in Buddhism many years ago while he was still living in mainland China. In 1948, when he realized that the Chinese communists were going to win the war, Chang decided he would have to leave mainland China and go to Taiwan. Those were hard times, and Chang was forced to choose between what to take with him and what to leave behind. Since he loved Buddhism more than anything, he decided to abandon most of his personal property and take as much Buddhist literature with him as he could. Accordingly, he packed many large crates full of Buddhist sutras and books and took them to Taiwan where eventually he opened the Chien K'ang Book Store.

Once in Taiwan, Chang became a publisher of Buddhist sutras and books

on Buddhism. He played an important part in having the Tripitaka published in Chinese. In 1957, Chang started *Awakening the World* magazine. His
intentions for the magazine were to form a link between Buddhist tradi-
tions and modern readers. Some years later, Chang turned the work of
publishing *Awakening the World* over to me. We still publish it today.

Chang was one of the first deep sources of modern Buddhist culture to
become active in Taiwan. His home was always full of Buddhist monks and
scholars. Many problems concerning the propagation of Buddhism in
Taiwan were solved by that group. Chang is over ninety years old today. He
has no children and, gradually, he has been forgotten by most Buddhists.
Whenever I think of him, I realize anew how grateful I am to him for all
that he did for Buddhism.

A few years ago I bought a house for him in the United States. We do
the best we can to take care of him. Every New Year's we bring him to Hsi
Lai Temple in Los Angeles to see the lanterns and celebrate with us.

Whenever I see Chang, I want to do even more for him. When I consider
all he has done for Buddhism, I wonder how can any of us ever repay him?

HELPING A HELPER

I first discovered Chu Chia-chun's talents as an
editor through the work he did on a magazine directed toward young
people who attended summer camps run by the government. Chu lived in
Ilan so I asked him to help with layout and editing of *Buddhism Today* and
Awakening the World magazines. His work on those publications was excellent. His layouts were fresh and new and his editorial decisions were very
successful in attracting new readers. His work was so good he quickly
became quite famous in magazine circles in Taiwan.

I still vividly remember Chu coming to Lei Yin Temple to do his work.
I used to get everything ready for him. I laid out glue, scissors, pens and
paper on the table. I made sure that his pillow and blankets for the night had
been freshly washed and ironed. I always folded them neatly and placed
them on his bed.

Chu usually stayed up very late working. During that time I always hovered around him, helping in any way I could. I used to bring him hot milk, noodles, and other snacks to keep him going. He often protested, saying, "Master, it's late. Why don't you go to bed? I'll be all right by myself." No matter what he said, I always stayed with him until he was finished with his work. If the weather were cold I would even give him my own blanket for the night.

Some of the people who knew what I was doing would ask me, "You are the master. Why do you treat one of your disciples as if you were his servant?"

I said, "He is putting so much energy into helping us propagate Buddhism, it is only right that I treat him with as much care and kindness as I can."

HIS CONTRIBUTION

Years ago, Chao Mao-lin was a chief of police in Chiangsu Province. After coming to Taiwan in 1949, he became head of the Taiwan Feather Manufacturer's Coop. Chao was also a Buddhist lay preacher. For over twenty years, he preached the Dharma in schools, temples and prisons. He was tireless in his efforts and he spoke wherever he was needed. He also preached the Dharma over the radio.

When he was young, Chao had learned to preach without using a microphone, so he had a deep, powerful voice that everybody was able to recognize immediately. His voice was clear and true, and he could chant the sutras better than most monks. When he became old, he came to live at Buddha's Light Mountain. We took good care of him during his last years. After he died, we sealed his ashes in the Tomb of Eternal Life. To this day, we burn incense for him morning and night and we conduct special ceremonies for him every spring and autumn. Once some devotees asked me why we were showing so much respect for Chao Mao-lin.

I answered, "We are just trying to honor someone who did a lot for Buddhism."

PAYING EXTRA FOR SHOES

In the summer of 1964, a man carried a big sack of Buddhist footwear into Shou Shan Temple where I was staying. He had brought the shoes to sell to the monks in the temple, and I could see that he had worked hard to get them there. The weather had been very hot, and his back was soaked with sweat when he arrived. At the time we were quite poor. There were not very many monks in Taiwan in those days and the business of selling us shoes couldn't have been all that good. When I asked him the price of a pair, he said, "One pair is thirty yuan." I took forty yuan out of my pocket and gave it to him for a pair of shoes. He lifted his head and looked at me strangely when he saw that I was giving him an extra ten yuan. He said, "Everybody else tries to bargain for a lower price, but you are giving me extra. Why is that?"

I said, "Selling shoes to monks is a tough business, but if you didn't do it, where would we get them? If you can make a little extra, then you will stay in business and continue bringing us shoes. I'm not thinking only of you when I give you extra money, I'm also thinking of myself."

"I've never heard anyone say anything like that before, " he replied, rubbing the back of his head in mild wonderment. Some time later, that same man sent his son to our temple to become a monk.

SOME CHILDREN NAMED LI

When Buddha's Light Mountain was first established, people sometimes would bring in a child who had been abandoned on the road. I felt sorry for the children and built a home and a school for them. We never knew who their parents were nor what the children's names were.

One day, the person in charge of caring for the children came to me and said, "Yesterday we tried to establish a family registry (a legal requirement in Taiwan) for those children, but since we didn't know their names, the registrar refused to accept our submissions. He said they have to have the name of someone who accepts responsibility for the children before they can enter them in the registry. Master, if the monastery accepts responsibility for them, maybe someday . . . There could be a problem with inheritance, or . . . some other sort of trouble . . . "

I could tell he was quite concerned about potential problems with the children so I said, "Then let's put them all in my family registry. They can take my family name, Li."

"Master!" he said. "You can't do that! What if . . . ?"

"Let's not worry about what might happen," I said. "In a sense, all children in the world are my children. And these are my children, too. If something happens in the future, well, then that's the way it will be."

He said nothing more. The next day he went back to register the children under my name.

From then on, I treated the children as if they were my own. I sent them to school, paid their bills, bought them clothing and school supplies. One day, a tourist saw the children and said, "How sad! They are so small and yet they have no parents." When I heard about that comment, I made a new rule that outsiders were not permitted in the children's area. I wanted to prevent anyone else from saying something that would hurt their feelings.

Who can say they have no parents? The children of the world are the responsibility of all of us. If we can succeed in loving them as if they were our own, then we will succeed in making everyone in the world part of our family.

The years have passed, and those children all are grown now. They have entered society and taken jobs, and now they, in turn, are able to help others.

ADDING PARENTS

For some reason, the Taiwanese identity card of Venerable Sheng Yen had never had his parents' names placed on it. Many years ago, Shen Chia-chen invited Venerable Sheng Yen to go to America. Sheng Yen made all of the preparations necessary to go to the United States, only to find out at the last moment that the American Consulate would not give him a visa due to a rule that stated that anyone whose birth circumstances were unclear would not be allowed a visa.

Feeling more than a little disturbed by this news, Sheng Yen went to the Taiwan authorities to ask for help. They told him, "There is no way we can add your parents' names to your card now."

That was in 1967 at the time when Buddha's Light Mountain was just being established. When I heard about Sheng Yen's problem, I remembered that the chief inspector for the Kaohsiung County Police Department, Chiang Chen-hsun, was a man who came from the same area of mainland China as I had. We both had grown up near Yangchou in Chiangsu Province. I knew that Chiang now oversaw identity papers for the whole county of Kaohsiung, Taiwan. I thought that he might be able to help us so I went to see him. I told to him how important it was for Sheng Yen to go to the United States, and I begged him to do everything he could to help us get his papers in order. When Chiang saw that he was being asked by an old friend from the same town where he had grown up, he called a lot of officials together to study Sheng Yen's case. One of them knew of a way of adding Sheng Yen's parents' names to his identity card without violating any laws. Once the names were added to his card, Sheng Yen was able to obtain the necessary visa. The affair ended simply, but it was only because I had grown up in a place so near to Chiang's old home town that we were able to finally get Sheng Yen his visa to go to the United States.

Over the years, I have often thought of Chiang Chen-hsun and the kindness he showed us. He helped us with a big problem and I have never ceased to feel grateful to him for it.

A MOUTHFUL OF GOOD TEETH

Over the years, many people have come to Buddha's Light Mountain to study Buddhism or enter the monastic order. Because of this, the cost of taking care of everybody has increased quite a lot. We have medical expenses, travel expenses, educational expenses, and the expenses of daily upkeep of the monastery. Some time ago, there was a period when the cost of dental care for the monastics was really getting out of hand. It was becoming our largest expense. One day our accountant came to me with a stack of bills and receipts for dental care. She raised her eyebrows in concern and said, "Master, recently there are too many people having dental work done. Costs are out of control. One treatment can go as high as ten thousand yuan. We simply cannot afford to continue spending money like this. It's a big burden."

I said, "Even if it is a big burden, we still have to spend the money."

She said, "You know, some of these people take so much from the monastery, but they never give anything back. In fact, once their teeth have been fixed, many of them leave the order. And then they criticize us. In my opinion, it's a waste of money to be helping them in the first place."

I said, "Even though they can't seem to use their mouths to say anything good about us, at least I know I've given them a mouthful of good teeth to say it with."

STANDING IN FOR BUDDHA
TO GIVE THANKS

Chang Chien-fen was an accomplished artist. Fine examples of his calligraphy and poetry hang in many Buddhist temples in Taiwan. In one of his poems he wrote:

The mercy of our ancestors is eternal
Now we are here, now we pray for them.
In truth, there is no hell anywhere except
In our hearts, where we create and we destroy it.

When Chang became old and sick, I learned that he was having trouble taking care of himself. To help him, I took money out of our food and clothing expenses to pay for the dialysis treatments he needed. Some people wondered why I was going to so much trouble for him. They asked, why do you want to help him so much? Why is your relationship so deep? The truth was, it didn't matter to me what kind of a relationship we had, or didn't have. It was simply because Chang had done so much for Buddhism that I felt the desire to help him as much as I could. It was my way of "standing in for the Buddha" to thank someone who had worked so hard for the good of his teachings. Chang's contributions were especially valuable because during the time he was composing poems and writing calligraphy for Buddhism, there were very few people who were able to do what he was doing. I thought we owed it to him to take care of him in his old age.

THE PRICE OF A BOWL OF NOODLES

Many years ago, I used to travel between Ilan and Kaohsiung to preach the Dharma and lecture on Buddhism. The trip took about ten hours each way. In those days, vegetarian restaurants in Taiwan were few and far between.

In the city of Changhua, I found a small place in a narrow little alley where I could stop for lunch and get plain soup noodles. The owner of the shop was a quiet man. I never once saw him speak a full sentence to any of the people who came in for lunch. He charged one and one-half yuan for a bowl of soup noodles. Whenever I ate there, I would tell him that his food was so good he should be charging five yuan for the noodles.

"If I charged five yuan a bowl," he would say, "no one would come here to eat anymore."

I said, "Maybe other people wouldn't come, but I still would."

I started to pay him five yuan for my noodles, but then after a while, he began refusing to take any money from me at all. I said, "Originally it was me who brought up the subject of the price of noodles. I said you should be charging five yuan a bowl. Why do you turn everything around now and accept nothing?" He never explained himself, and I would always have to force him to accept payment for my lunch.

Before long, thirty years had gone by. The cook has built a high rise building where his old shop had stood. He is wealthy enough to retire, but since he has the habit of working, he continues to go to his new shop and make noodles every day. With all the changes in Taiwan's economy, a big change has come in the price of a bowl of noodles at his shop. Now a bowl of soup noodles sells for thirty yuan. The price is fair and the food is still good, so his business is just as good as it always was. And he's just the same as he always was, too. He is still solemn and quiet as he stands in the steam wafting around his stove. Whenever he sees me coming, however, he becomes quite lively and animated as he walks out front to greet me.

TAKING REFUGE OVER THE PHONE

When we first started building Buddha's Light University, we raised money for the school by selling artwork that had been donated to us. Our efforts received a lot of public attention and many people helped us, so every time we had a sale, we were very successful. One day, Ch'en Hsiao-chun, who was in charge of publicity for the sales, brought two of her friends by to see me. Her friends wanted to volunteer some of their time toward helping us. As we talked together, the two said that they were amazed that we had been so successful in getting so many high-quality works of art together for our sales. I took out a painting by Chang Ta-ch'ien (a very famous twentieth-century Chinese painter) called "Kuan Yin Bodhisattva" and proceeded to use it to illustrate one way we acquired paintings.

One evening, as the wind blew softly under a white moon, I sat beside my window to read a stack of letters. One of the letters in the stack caught my attention. The letter was from someone named Kao Po-chen. Kao said his father, Kao Ling-mei, had taken ill and been sent to the hospital. Now that he was in the hospital, Ling-mei had expressed the wish to become a Buddhist. The Kaos lived in Hong Kong. At the end of his letter, Po-chen asked me if it would be possible for me to travel to Hong Kong to grant his father's wish? I was very touched that Po-chen wanted to help his father so much that he would send a letter like that to me.

It's a bit of journey to Hong Kong from Taiwan, and, as there was no time in my schedule, I knew I would not be able to make the trip. I decided to do the refuge ceremony over the phone, instead. When we had finished with the ceremony, the entire Kao family was so grateful they decided to donate a painting to Buddha's Light Mountain. The painting turned out to be the one by Chang Ta-ch'ien. All along, Mr. Kao had been one of Hong Kong's most famous art collectors.

LEAVE NO ONE BEHIND

When the Shami Novice Training School was first established at Buddha's Light Mountain in 1967, some of the students we took in were very difficult to control because they came from homes where there had been a lot of problems. The Buddha taught that we should not leave anyone behind, so I took in anyone who wanted to come to class. Those kids misbehaved a lot and they didn't like to study, but they were playful and better at games than most students.

Some of our teachers said that they were good for nothing but trouble and that they had no appreciation for what we were doing for them. They suggested that it would be better to send them back home. I said, "Let me try teaching them then."

I gave them essays to copy, and while they were working, I would praise them to make them feel good. From their copying, they learned how to read and write. Over time they got better at their school work. Once they got an article published in *Awakening the World* magazine, and they very proudly came to show it to me.

After the basketball court was built, we played together every day. With practice they came to understand the game and through that they began to learn how to follow rules and have respect for other people and how to function as a member of a team.

Without formal training, those same students eventually became excellent electricians and plumbers. We used them for lots of work that was done at Buddha's Light Mountain. Their work was so good that workers who came in from outside the monastery often would praise the way that they had done something.

One day, one of those students rode his motorcycle down the hill to buy some plumbing supplies. On the way, he was hit by a car and knocked unconscious. He was taken to the emergency room. When he opened his eyes for the first time, he looked around, and then the first thing he said was, "Please tell Master Hsing Yun that I am all right."

Who can say now that those kids are good for nothing but trouble and that they have no sense of gratitude?

KITCHEN WORK

Over twenty years ago, a group of nine young people came to Buddha's Light Mountain for a visit. They arrived at around two o'clock in the afternoon on a hot summer day. They were tired and hungry. One of them told the woman behind the receptionist's desk, "We are college students on summer vacation and we've come all the way from the north of Taiwan to visit Buddha's Light Mountain. Since this is our first visit, we got lost on the way. Now that we are here, we've noticed that we've missed lunch. I'm sorry, but we are really hungry. Is there any way we can get something to eat?"

Arrangements were made for one of the nuns in the temple to prepare some noodles for them. Just about that time, I was finishing up meeting with some guests. I came around the back way from the meeting room and noticed the group of students eating in the dining hall. They were literally attacking their food as if they were starving. As I looked closer, I saw that all they had was a small bowl of noodles each. They were young and healthy boys, and I thought to myself that's not nearly enough food for them. I went straight to the kitchen and fried a big plate of rice and vegetables to add to their meal.

When the steaming food was brought to their table, they looked somewhat surprised because they hadn't expected to see any more food. As they looked around, one of them said, "How much will this be?"

"You don't have to pay anything for it," the woman who was caring for them said. "This food was prepared by the abbot of this temple as a gift for all of you."

Later, when it was time for them to leave, they donated nine hundred yuan to Buddha's Light Mountain. At the time, that was a lot of money for a group of college students. The woman who received the money was very pleased with it, and she came straight to me to report what had happened. The truth is, all I had wanted to do was feed some tired young people. I had not been looking to get paid back ten times what the food was worth. In preaching the Dharma, often it's the little things that touch me the most. What made me happiest on that day was looking out the window and seeing those nine students as they left. They were dancing and jumping and laughing with joy as they went down the stairs.

THE PRICE OF MASTER'S CALLIGRAPHY

In the spring of 1994, an auction was held in Taipei to raise money for Buddha's Light University Foundation Fund. Most of what we sold in the auction were artworks and among them were some examples of my calligraphy. When those came up for sale, you could feel the mood of the audience rise as each bid went higher than the last.

"Twenty thousand yuan,". . . "Sixty thousand yuan,". . . "One hundred thousand yuan. . . "

In the crowd there was a man who had brought his young son along with him to enjoy the day. As people called out numbers and the bidding went higher and higher, the boy turned his little head back and forth with a look of great concern. He had a one hundred yuan bill squeezed tightly in his small hand. Just after someone bid two hundred thousand yuan, there was a momentary lull in the room and the boy, in his tiny voice yelled out, "one hundred yuan!"

When the crowd heard the sound of his high little voice calling out, the room fell completely silent.

"I won't sell it for two hundred thousand yuan," I said. "But I will sell it for one hundred yuan to my little friend here."

The boy's name was Wang Ping. When I said I would sell the calligraphy to him, his face burst into smiles, and everybody in the room applauded.

A LITTLE DANDELION

I've been preaching the Dharma for many years, and I've met with a lot of success and praise. I've also received many expensive and wonderful gifts. But of everything I've ever been given, the gift that moved me the most was a little dandelion a little girl gave me one day in northwestern India.

A large crowd of people had gathered to say goodbye to us. People were everywhere. In the crowd, I caught a glimpse of a little girl holding a little dandelion. Her small lips were pursed as she shyly looked toward me. The goodbye ceremony ended, and at last we got in our car. Just as we were starting to drive away, the little girl with the dandelion raced up to us and pushed her little flower in between my window and the car door. I begged the driver to stop so I could give her a small string of prayer beads. As I gave her the beads, her face broke into the most beautiful smile, then her little eyes brimmed and overflowed with tears.

As our car moved forward again, the yellow dandelion on the window gently shook in the breeze. In our rearview mirror, I could see the little girl still standing behind us. Her tiny body was straight and motionless. Her hands were pressed together before her in the traditional Indian gesture. As I watched her figure slowly grow smaller, my heart exploded with love.

KINDNESS

Several years ago, a group of us traveled to Japan. We got off a train in Tokyo and went outside to look for the bus we needed to take. We climbed on what we thought was the right bus, but after speaking with the driver, we learned that it was not.

The driver said, "This bus won't take you there. You need to go around the corner over there and down the street to find the bus you want."

This was our first trip to Japan, so none of us knew where the driver was telling us to go. We felt quite lost, but there was nothing else to do but get off the bus and try to fend for ourselves. We thanked the driver and went outside. Our confusion must have shown in our faces, because in a moment the driver turned to the people already sitting in the bus and said, "I'm very sorry, but I have to show these people where to catch their bus. Please wait a moment for me. I'll be right back."

Then he turned off the engine of the bus, pulled out the keys and jumped down to the street. He guided us along a confusing route for about five minutes until we arrived at the correct stop.

A few years later, I went to Japan again to preach the Dharma. After one of my talks, a young Japanese came up to me to say hello. He was quite excited as he said, "You couldn't possibly remember me, but I remember you. Can you recall a time a few years ago when you were in Tokyo and a bus driver shut off his engine to walk you to your stop? I was one of the passengers on that bus."

"Oh!" I said. "I'm sorry we made all of you wait for so long!"

"Oh, no!" the young man said. "Don't say that! This is a Buddhist country and we all understand the importance of helping others.

"Can you guess what happened when the driver came back to the bus?" he continued. "As soon as he came back in the door, everyone on the bus started clapping their hands in approval."

A THIRTY-YEAR WAIT

In 1949, when I first came to Taiwan, I spent some time in Keelung, a port city in northern Taiwan. I remember walking past a temple one day and stopping for a moment to look through one of its windows. Inside, I saw a Buddhist nun looking back at me. I was very young at the time and too shy to just walk in and introduce myself. Instead, I turned away and walked on. Some time later, I learned that the nun I had seen through the window was Master Hsiu Hui. She was so respected in Keelung, people called her the "Great Hero Among Women." Her temple was the famous Chi Le Temple.

Thirty years later, when she became head of the Keelung Buddhist Association, Hsiu Hui came to Universal Gate Temple in Taipei to look for me. During our conversation, she said she had always remembered our brief encounter of thirty years before. At that time, she had wanted to ask me to come into the temple, and take up preaching the Dharma there, but it had taken another thirty years before our karma had brought us together again. She continued to tell me that she felt very grateful for everything Buddha's Light Mountain had done for Buddhism in Taiwan, and that her heart told her that the humanistic Buddhism we were preaching was just what the world needed. Then she offered to give Chi Le Temple to Buddha's Light Mountain. I considered her offer, but I knew we already were short-handed. Since I was afraid we would not be able to care for it properly, I told her I would have to refuse. I then invited her to visit Buddha's Light Mountain.

Not long after that, she did come to Buddha's Light Mountain for a visit. She walked around the mountain for a while and then told me that she wanted to make a vow. She said she wanted to join the monastic order at Buddha's Light Mountain and remain in it for the rest of her life. I was so deeply moved by her sincerity that I instantly granted her request.

Chi Le Temple in Keelung was famous for its excellent location and for the great contributions it had made to Buddhism. When word got out that Hsiu Hui had donated the temple to Buddha's Light Mountain, she met with a great deal of opposition from many people involved with the temple. Hsiu Hui was unwavering in her determination, though, and before long, Chi Le Temple became a branch temple of Buddha's Light Mountain. Along with the temple building, she also donated all money held by the temple to me to be used for preaching the Dharma. To fulfill my responsibilities toward her, I appointed some devotees to oversee refurbishing the temple. Later, we established a Buddhist college there.

The day Hsiu Hui gave me Chi Le Temple she was eighty years old. I remember her saying with great happiness, "I have waited thirty years for this day. And now my wish has been granted!"

BUYING A WATCH

During some free time in Japan one day, some of us went out to buy a few presents for devotees in Taiwan. In one duty-free gift shop, I saw a beautiful watch which I was interested in buying. The proprietor of the shop told me the watch cost twenty thousand yen.

I said, "Isn't there a rule in this country that tourists are supposed to be given a discount at duty-free stores like this?"

"Oh! You are right!" he said. "I had almost forgotten! After the discount that same watch will be eighteen thousand yen. Can I see your passport, please? I need your passport number to give you the discount."

"I'm sorry," I said. "I have forgotten my passport. We just came out for a while. My passport is still in the hotel." I knew it would take too long to go back to the hotel to get my passport, so I said, "Let's forget about the discount. I'll pay the full twenty thousand for the watch."

He surprised me when he replied, "No, we shouldn't do that. The government has said that you should get a discount and therefore you should get a discount. I know what we can do! Tell me your hotel address, and someone from this store will deliver the watch to you before you go back to Taiwan."

The night before we were to leave, the man himself showed up at my room, just as he had promised. I showed him my passport and paid for the watch. Then I thanked him for the trouble he had gone to. His face was still perspiring from the exertion of having come to my room. I felt bad about just letting him go out the door again without showing him any hospitality, so I asked him to come in and have a glass of tea with me before starting back to his store.

We sat and talked for a while. I thanked him again for going to the trouble of bringing me the watch. Then he reached into his breast pocket and pulled out a copy of the *Heart Sutra*. He pointed to the part which said, "There is nothing to attain, and thus the Bodhisattva. . ."

As he pointed at the sutra in his hand, he looked at me and said, "I have nothing to attain. In the midst of nothing, I have everything. I did not seek to attain anything by bringing you that watch."

His smile was so tranquil and sincere, I encouraged him to say more.

"The most important thing I have learned in life," he continued, "is that joy can always be found by doing what you are supposed to do when you are supposed to do it. And true joy can only be found there."

RECUPERATION AND FRUIT

In 1995, I had open-heart surgery. After the operation, I spent a few weeks in the hospital recuperating. The first day after my surgery, I opened my eyes to see the hazy image of an old woman going from bed to bed mopping the floor. In order to show my appreciation for her efforts at keeping the room clean, and to not miss a chance to make a new friend, I made an attempt to move my arms. I wanted to reach up and get some small things near me, but I didn't have the strength to do it.

Just then, I noticed a basket of fruit on a table at the foot of my bed. I said to the attendant near me, "Please give that woman a piece of fruit."

"What fruit?" he said. "Fruit is not allowed in here while people are recuperating."

"Isn't that fruit right over there?" I asked.

It wasn't. It turned out that what I thought was a basket of fruit was actually an oil painting given me by Chang Chin-sheng.

I failed in my efforts to give the old woman something that day, but during the remaining few weeks I spent in the hospital, I was able to give many things away. When people brought me fruit and flowers, I quickly turned them over to others, and in that way, all of us were able to deepen our awareness of our karmic interrelatedness.

I SEE ALL OF YOU

When I had heart surgery in 1995, I didn't want anyone to worry about me so I kept things as quiet as I could. Word of the operation slipped out anyway, though, and as I was recuperating, I received many cards and letters and phone calls and gifts. In order to thank everyone for their concern, I hosted a get-together at Chung Shan Hall in Taipei in May.

During his speech at the event, Cheng Shih-yen told a Ch'an story.

"Once," he said, "Ch'an Master Tung Shan became quite ill and was forced to take to his bed. When his disciple, Tsao Shan, saw him lying there, he asked, 'Master, your body seems to be ill. Do you in some sense have a healthy body, too?'

"Tung Shan replied, 'I do.'

"Tsao Shan continued, 'Is your healthy body able to see you, Master?'

"Tung Shan said, 'I am looking at it right now.'

"Tsao Shan did not understand and asked again, 'But what is it you are seeing?'

"Tung Shan said, 'When I look, I see no illness at all.'"

Then Cheng turned his head and asked me, "Master, when you were ill, what did you see?"

I said, "I saw all of you."

A RESOLUTION FOR 2/28*

I first heard about the "2/28 Incident" when I came to Taiwan in 1949. The "2/28 Incident" was very disturbing to me, and I've tried hard to think of some way to lessen the pain and resentment caused by the tragedy.

In the early 1980s, I recommended that the government clear the names of those who had been killed in the incident. It wasn't until 1991, however, that conditions were right to do something to heal those old wounds. When the Chinese chapter of Buddha's Light International Association was established in Taiwan, we conducted a ceremony for those who had been killed.

* On February 28, 1947, thousands of Taiwanese were killed by Kuomintang troops. The origins of the incident are unclear, but the "2/28 Incident" caused a long-lasting rift between native-born Taiwanese and mainland Chinese, who made up the vast majority of Kuomintang troops and officers. At the time, the Kuomintang said the incident was an "insurrection," while most native-born Taiwanese considered it to be a massacre.

Both government officials and the families of those killed were present at the ceremony. Later, the remains of those who had been killed were inurned in Buddha's Light Mountain's Tomb of Eternal Life. Regular services still are held in their memory. I hope these efforts will be of some help in healing those old wounds and allow people in Taiwan to move forward in a spirit of forgiveness and mutual acceptance.

In 1994, we hosted the "2/28 Memorial Music Concert" in Taipei. During a speech I gave at the concert, I begged everyone to put the past behind them and move forward toward a world of peace and prosperity. After coming down from the stage, President Lee Teng-hui, who happened to have a seat next to mine, complimented me on what I had said. He said my words had been very appropriate to the situation. The truth was, though, all I had done was speak from my heart.

DISCIPLES

LITTLE NOVICES SLEEPING

Many of the students in our Shami Novice Training School are quite young. They are at an age where playing is everything and studying is something to be avoided, if possible. Often, they sleep in class, too. Some of them even sleep all day, right from the first period to the sixth period. That kind of behavior can be more than a little disturbing to their teachers.

One day, Venerable Hui Hsing, who taught T'ien T'ai Buddhism, came to me. He was quite angry with his students and he said, "If you don't expel those kids who sleep all day, I will refuse to teach anymore!"

I tried to calm him down. "Slow down and think about this," I said. "Those children are at an age where playing is all they think about. It's not in their natures to enjoy studying. If they just show up for class, we can say that they are doing some good for themselves. If they manage to sleep for six hours in a row, I think that's quite an achievement!"

Venerable Hui Hsing burst out laughing when I finished talking. I continued, "Even though those children are sleeping, their minds are dreaming within the embrace of the Buddha. If they wake up for a minute here or there, they might hear a few words, or a sentence. Those words might help them for the rest of their lives. Isn't that much better than spending their days somewhere else, learning to develop bad habits?"

A GOOD METHOD

When Venerable Yi Te first entered the monastic order, some of her old habits stayed with her for a while. Before she had become a nun, she was fond of eggs, and that fondness stayed with her even after she put on the robes.

She loved eggs so much that she often went back home to visit her family just so she could have some. Since we are strict vegetarians, eggs normally are never served in the monastery. One day, I heard that she was planning to go home yet again to have some eggs. I asked Yang Ts'e-man (a lay follower who had served in the monastery for many years) to make a lot of eggs for her. Make every kind you can think of, I said. She made boiled eggs, fried eggs, stewed eggs, poached eggs, and scrambled eggs.

At the same time, I let it be known that I was not going to permit Yi Te to go home for the visit she had requested.

When Yi Te heard that I was not going to let her go home, she came looking for me. When she found me, I told her to go see Yang Ts'e-man first and then come back and talk to me. When she found Yang Ts'e-man, she also found a whole table spread with every kind of egg dish we could think of. She tasted some of them, but from that day on she saw her own desire for eggs as something to be more careful about.

At the time, some people were critical of what I had done, but after a while most of them came to see that giving her all those eggs had not been such a bad thing to do. If doing something like that can really succeed in turning someone around, then it's a good method. It's the right thing to do. I think there are a lot of problems in this world that should be solved more or less like this. We don't need to be so rigid in our beliefs and expectations. If we can be just a little more tolerant and open-minded when it come to dealing with others, many things that look like problems will simply disappear of themselves.

ICE CAPADES

Twenty years ago, when I was chancellor of Buddha's Light Mountain Buddhist College, the Ice Capades were scheduled to come to Kaohsiung. The whole city was excited. One of the students at our college, Liao Hsiu-chi, became especially excited about the prospect of seeing them—or not seeing them, as it were.

"If I can't go, I will regret it for the rest of my life," she told one of her classmates. The problem was that we had a rule at our school that students were not allowed to leave campus during scheduled class times.

On the day of the show, I asked her to come to my office. I said, "I want you to help me with a few things. Please go to Kaohsiung and buy some office supplies for us. There will be three hundred yuan left over after you have gotten everything. You can use that money for anything you want, and it's okay if you return a little bit late. You don't need to go ask any of your teachers for permission."

She laughed out loud, and smiling from ear to ear, said, "Thank you, thank you, Chancellor. I understand your meaning."

After that day, she became one of our best students.

NYLON STOCKINGS

Huang Hsiu-mei was a beautiful and intelligent girl with a marvelous sense of humor. During the time when she was a student at Buddha's Light Mountain Buddhist College, however, she trailed just a trace of the dust of the world behind her.

Someone once asked her, "Hsiu-mei, are you planning to become a nun?"
She responded innocently, "But I have never worn nylon stockings!"

Sometime later, when I was in the United States, I asked someone to buy a few pairs of nylon stockings for me. As I went through customs on my way back to Taiwan, the customs agent looked strangely at me as if he wanted to say, "These nylon stockings are not illegal, but what in the world are they doing in your luggage? What does a monk need with these?" He didn't actually say anything, and I didn't say anything, but in my heart I answered him, "These stockings are for a wonderful young girl who has been captivated by an innocent dream. Don't you know that we monastics have just the same feelings as mothers and fathers?"

TURNING WEAPONS INTO
JADE AND SILK

Ts'ai Meng-hua works in the editing department at Buddha's Light Mountain. Once she sent me a very emotional letter which described how her father, Ts'ai Ch'ao-feng, had come to be a Buddhist.

Her father has six daughters and he loves them all very deeply. Some years ago, his oldest daughter, against the objections of both her parents, entered the monastic order at Buddha's Light Mountain. Her name is Man Wei. Soon after Man Wei put on the robes, her younger sister also became a nun at Buddha's Light Mountain. Her name is Chueh K'uan.

When both daughters joined the order so soon after one another, their father became very upset. He went to court to try to get them back. After a while though, he came to understand that they were committed to Buddhism, and his attitude toward them softened once more. Though he learned to accept his girls again, a kind of wall against Buddha's Light Mountain grew up around his heart, and behind that wall he developed a bitterness toward me that was not easy to overcome. This condition grew even worse when his third daughter, Meng-hua, began working as a lay disciple in the editing department at Buddha's Light Mountain.

In 1993, Meng-hua's grandmother died. Everyone was very sad. In an absent-minded moment, Mr. Ts'ai sighed, "It would be nice if Master Hsing Yun would come here now."

"Incredible! Suddenly my father wanted the very man who had had such a bad influence on his daughters to come visit his home!" Meng-hua wrote.

When Meng-hua heard him say that, she was overjoyed. However, she knew my schedule was irregular and that I often traveled abroad to preach the Dharma, so she was more than a little afraid that the opportunity for me to visit her father might be missed.

Just at that time, I returned to Taiwan from a trip abroad. When I heard about what had happened at the Ts'ais, I made room in my schedule to go to their small village, Tung Kang, to preside over the funeral for Meng-hua's grandmother. In her letter to me, Meng-hua wrote that she will never forget the moment I stepped into their house. Her father's eyes slowly filled with tears when he saw me, but what moved Meng-hua even more was that her father kneeled before me to pay his respects for my having come to his home. As he knelt, I told him, "We are all family here. Please don't treat me like a stranger."

Over the last few years, the wall that Mr. Ts'ai erected around his heart has slowly come down, revealing that all along there had been an immensely kind and tender being just behind it. He has brought thirty-seven of his relatives to Buddha's Light Mountain to take refuge in Buddhism. In 1995, he became head of the Tung Kang Buddha's Light Association.

One day, Meng-hua asked her father, "What is it that made you change so much? Why did you decide to take refuge in Buddhism?"

He answered, "Master Hsing Yun is a monk, but he is warm and kind. Our family can never repay him for what he has done for us."

At the end of her letter, Meng-hua wrote, "Master, thank you so much for your kindness. Now we have become a complete Buddhist family. With all my heart, I bow before you!"

If Meng-hua hadn't reminded me of those events, I would have already forgotten them. All my life I have simply tried to make other people feel happy. My efforts have been small, but so much has happened because of them. Now we have a whole family who have become Buddhists. In this world, we really can find warmth and kindness if we are willing to just look for them!

SYMPATHY

Ko Pen-chieh was from Hopei Province. He graduated from Peiyang University. During his life he was a great Buddhist. For many years he was the vice-chancellor of the American Buddhist Association's translation department in Taiwan. He was also a professor at Tung Hai University and Ch'eng Kung University. Among the works he translated is *Teachings of the Buddha*. He was one of the editors of the sixteen-volume *Buddha's Light Tripitaka*. He expended a lot of energy to further Buddhist culture in Taiwan and the world. Ko only gave to Buddhism and never asked for anything in return. He was the same way with people. When he became old, I asked him and his wife to come live at Buddha's Light Mountain.

On September 2, 1991, Ko died just when I was in the hospital myself after having broken my leg in a fall. As soon as I heard the news, I got myself into a wheelchair and went to his funeral. I wanted to burn some incense for him, at the least. When his wife, Chou T'en, saw me, she prostrated herself before me. After she had risen to her feet again, she said, "I was born in a palace and raised as a Manchurian princess. In my whole life I have only bowed like that to the emperor and to my parents. But now I have done it before you, too."

WIND AND RAIN
INCREASED HIS FAITH

In June, 1995, I heard that the oldest son of Huang Ying-chi was getting married. Huang was the principal of Sze Wei High School in Hualien, Taiwan. His son, Haung Wen-k'uei, was head doctor of Ho P'ing Hospital in Taipei. Huang was marrying a woman named Cheng Hsiu-feng, who was an English teacher in Tainan, Taiwan. Their wedding was going to be held at Buddha's Light Mountain.

The wedding came shortly after I had had heart surgery, and the weather was ferocious. A massive typhoon was blowing across Taiwan. Though I was still recuperating from my operation, I decided to travel from Taipei to Kaohsiung to preside over the ceremony. I wanted to do that because Huang Ying-chi had been an active member of Buddha's Light Mountain for a long time.

When he saw me arrive for his son's wedding, he said, "The wind and rain really do bring out the best in us. Here you are recuperating from your operation, but still you have come. This wind and rain has increased the faith of my whole family!"

The next day, Huang Ying-chi brought a large donation to me as a way of saying thanks for having come to his son's wedding. I knew he meant well, but I refused his offer, saying, "Do you think I came from Taipei for money?"

When he heard me say that, I could see he was deeply moved. He said, "Master, from this day on, I will dedicate even more energy to Buddhism and even more energy to helping Buddha's Light Mountain."

AN UNINVITED FRIEND

Hu Hsiu-ch'ing is now head of the Women's Chinese Medicine Association. When she was younger, she was a radio announcer who was famous for her beautiful voice. Her manner was refined and elegant, and she always was courteous with everyone. She was a devout Buddhist and, though she was not a disciple of mine, I had great respect for her. Every year for twenty years, she was master of ceremonies at the annual Buddhist lecture series we held in Taipei.

Hu was an adopted child. When her birth mother died one day, she was deeply affected and went immediately to Taichung to help with the funeral arrangements. As soon as I learned what had happened, I left to join them, driving all night to arrive in Taichung just in time to attend the funeral. I wanted to show my appreciation to Hu for all that she had done for Buddhism.

In the course of a year, it's normal for many people to ask me to attend ceremonies of all kinds. I usually find someone else to go in my place. I decline many invitations. But in Hu's case, even though I had not been asked, I went anyway, as an uninvited friend.

LI KU

One day in 1977, I was going to a class at Buddha's Light Mountain when I saw an old woman walking slowly in the distance. She was very small and bent over and she squinted at the ground as she moved. Her tiny feet had been bound when she was a girl so it required a lot of effort for her to walk. I hurried to catch up to her.

"Madam," I said. "Please come inside and rest for a while. Let me give you some tea."

She didn't respond to my words, but only continued walking as if she had heard nothing. I thought to myself, maybe she can't understand my accent. It was clear to me from the way she was heading that soon she would have to descend the long staircase below Non-Duality Gate. I ran right up beside her and spoke again, "Madam, there are more than one hundred steps ahead. It is a difficult descent. There's an easier way over here. Please let me take you that way, okay?"

This time she came with me. After I had shown her the way, we said goodbye. Several years later, while I was in Malaysia preaching the Dharma, I got a call from that same woman. She wanted to come see me. I was very busy at that time, so our visit together was quite hurried. Nevertheless, during the middle of it, she pressed a brown paper bag into my hands, saying, "This is for your educational fund." Then she turned and left without saying anything more. I opened the bag. Inside, there was eight hundred thousand yuan.

After that, whenever I went to Malaysia to preach the Dharma, she would donate two or three hundred thousand yuan at a time. I can't even remember how many times she gave to us. I've heard since that many other Buddhist organizations approached her asking for money, but that she never gave anything to any of them. Once, someone asked her why she was willing to donate to Buddha's Light Mountain and not to other organizations. She replied, "Because Master Hsing Yun is good at preaching the Dharma. And there's another reason: once I visited Buddha's Light Mountain in Taiwan. He didn't know me at all then, and I know that I looked like any other tired old lady on a hot day. But Master Hsing Yun treated me very well. I know he is kind and warm-hearted, even to strangers. Eventually, I plan to give him everything I have."

Her name was Li Ku.

FRIENDSHIP BASED ON A BOOK

One day a man named Lin Hsi-sung came to Universal Gate Temple in Taipei. Just as he was coming up, I was going out. We bumped into each other outside the elevator. Lin said to me, "Aren't you Master Hsing Yun? I've come because I want to buy a copy of *Buddhist Temples of Taiwan* from you."

I thought, "That was really not my book. All I did was write the preface for it and it has been quite a few years since then. I know the book is out of print. I wonder if I can possibly find a copy for him?"

Out loud I said, "Please wait a moment. I will go look for it."

I got lucky and found my last copy on the edge of my bookcase. When I gave it to Lin, he reached in his pocket and pulled out six hundred yuan to pay me for the book. I refused his money. "Let's use this book to start a new friendship, instead," I said. He was happy with that idea and returned home.

Two months later, he came to see me again. He said, "I've heard that you are going to be preaching the Dharma for three days at Sun Yat-sen Memorial Hall. I've also heard that each day you will be giving away five thousand copies of your collected teachings. That's really a big burden for you. Why not let me print all those books and give them away for you?" That act of kindness cost him a lot, yet he told me that he was happy to do it. He felt it was a way of repaying me for having given him *Buddhist Temples of Taiwan*.

From that time on, he often came to Universal Gate Temple to pay his respects to the Buddha and to listen to Dharma talks. I heard one time that when Universal Gate Temple was suddenly in need of money, he loaned us over three million yuan. He also stipulated that we need repay the loan only if he became destitute unexpectedly. Otherwise, there would be no need to repay any of it. Recently, he has moved with his wife to Los Angeles, and I've heard that they often volunteer their time to help at Hsi Lai Temple.

A THIRTY-YEAR PROMISE

One evening in early winter as the colors of sunset were spreading across the sky, I saw a familiar face out of the corner of my eye. I was behind the main Buddha Hall at the time, starting to go up the stairs. I knew it was her. Forty years ago she had become one of my disciples. "Weng Chueh-hua!" I called out. She turned and looked at me, but her eyes were full of tears and she was unable to speak.

The next morning, I saw her again. She put a piece of paper into my hand. It said:

> A donation of five hundred thousand yuan.
> Weng Chueh-hua, from
> Chin Shan Temple, bows to you.

Even though she had written only a few words, I was deeply moved. I asked her, "It's been thirty years now. Do you have any regrets?"

"No," she said. "I have been more than willing to do as you asked."

Thirty years ago, when I moved to the south of Taiwan to preach the Dharma, I begged Chueh-hua not to go with me. I wanted her to stay in Taipei to continue serving at Chin Shan Temple. She had done what I asked and stayed there for thirty years.

Think about it: how many of us can speak a promise of just a few words, and then honor that promise for thirty years?

THEY CAME FOR THE DHARMA

Kao Ch'eng-yi had some belief in Buddhism, but he never really thought about it very deeply. When he was a director at Taiwan Power Company many years ago, he would invite monks from

Buddha's Light Mountain to come to his workplace every summer to perform a Buddhist ceremony and chant sutras.

Some years later, his daughter decided to become a nun at Buddha's Light Mountain. Her monastic name is Chueh San. After she became a nun, her family became more interested in Buddhism and their faith increased. Whenever we have a public gathering at Buddha's Light Mountain, Mr. and Mrs. Kao always join in.

In 1994, we held a meeting for relatives of monastics at Buddha's Light Mountain. By the time the Kaos arrived, it was already 8:00 P.M. and the guest house was full. By the time I heard about their problem, it was already 11:00 P.M. I asked the Kaos to come to Dharma Hall to have some tea with me. As we were visiting, I learned that they had not had any dinner that night. I found some bread for them to tide them over, and we arranged for them to spend the rest of the night in a sitting room attached to one of our offices.

The next day, I went to see how they had spent the night. They didn't show any sign of feeling slighted by having been given such poor accommodations. Instead, they were all smiles and very happy as they greeted me. "We came for the Dharma," they explained, "not for the accommodations."

A LOVING AND
RESPECTFUL DISCIPLE

Thirty years ago, when I was head of the Ilan Buddhist Chanting Assembly, a man named Li Wu-yen often attended our services. Li was a radiologist at Jung Min Hospital at the time. Nowadays, he works for a private company which produces medical supplies. Since he has seen so much disease and death in his life that he has become very compassionate toward the sufferings of others.

For thirty years he has always been considerate to me. He frequently calls me to ask how I am doing. If I mention any problems, he always offers to help. Starting about ten years ago, he began trying to persuade me to go to a doctor for a check up. I always told him I was too busy with my work to see a doctor. One day he came to me personally and knelt before me to beg me to go for a medical check-up. I was so moved by his concern that I could not refuse him any longer.

In 1991, I fell while I was in the bathroom and broke my leg. As soon as Li heard what had happened, he made all the arrangements necessary for me to have my leg operated on and the bone set. He stayed close beside me before and after the operation to make sure everything went as it should. When I had open-heart surgery in 1995, he took time off from work and was at my side twenty-four hours a day. One of the first sights I saw when I opened my eyes after the operation was Li standing near my bed making sure that all was going well. I was deeply moved and very much comforted by his concern. I wonder how many people in today's world would even show their own parents this much love and respect?

Stories About

ANIMALS

IF IT HADN'T BEEN FOR THE DOG

One day about twenty years ago, just as the rain was stopping, Ko Wen-cho heard the screeching sound of car brakes, followed by the pained yelp of a dog.

Ko, who was just returning home after a day of teaching, wheeled his bicycle toward the sound and peddled quickly to the end of the street. Just around the corner, he saw a brown dog lying on its side in a large and growing pool of blood. The dog's intestines were spilling out of a hole in its abdomen and its back leg was crushed. Its body was trembling uncontrollably, and though the scene was difficult to look at, Ko tore off his jacket and used it to wrap the creature up. Then he got back on his bicycle and raced with the animal to a veterinarian's office that was not too far away.

The vet saved the dog's life, but it had come very close to dying. Even after Ko took him home, the weakened animal still required around-the-clock attention, which Ko's family administered as best they could by taking turns looking after him.

Apparently, the Kos cared for him well because pretty soon the dog started to recover his health. Before long, he was jumping and wiggling around their house as if nothing ever had happened. The Kos were delighted with the new addition to their family, and they named the dog Hsiao Hua, which means "Little Flower."

Some time later, on a quiet Sunday morning, Mr. Ko opened the front gate to his home and inadvertently let Hsiao Hua slip past him. The dog raced down the street with Mr. Ko following as closely behind him as he could. Suddenly, the dog stopped running and began scratching and barking at the front gate of house No. 7. It turned out that No. 7 was the home of the dog's former owners, the Ts'ais.

From that day on, the Kos' oldest daughter became good friends with the Ts'ais' oldest son. They knew each other through high school, college, and during a time when they both studied abroad. After about ten years of friendship, the two decided to marry.

Both families were delighted at how things turned out, and everyone was fully aware that if it hadn't been for Hsiao Hua, none of it ever would have happened.

RAISING A MONKEY

In 1956, I opened the Buddhist Tz'u Ai Nursery School in Ilan, Taiwan. People seemed to like what we were doing, and every day more students came to attend. At one time, we had as many as two hundred children in the school. To help them develop a sense of compassion for others, we set aside a small part of the grounds to raise birds and one monkey.

Our monkey was very playful and headstrong. Even Lu Ta-fu, who fed the animal every day, was unable to control him. The monkey, however, was afraid of me for some reason. Whenever he started acting up, all I would have to do is go stand in front of his cage and he would bow his head and quiet down again.

One day, I was in Lei Yin Temple next door to the school, conducting a Buddhist ceremony. We were just about to begin circling the Buddha when a teacher from the school ran in and nervously said, "The monkey has escaped. He's run across the street and climbed to the roof of a building. He won't listen to any of us and no one can catch him. What if someone gets hurt?"

I went with him to see what I could do. I shouted once at the monkey and he turned and squirreled his way directly back to his cage.

A keeper of a pet store who knew about our monkey often used to tell me not to give him water to drink. If you give him water, the man said, the monkey will grow up too quickly and stop being so much fun to play with. I never did what he suggested because I couldn't bear to let the animal go thirsty. As the monkey grew, I began to feel that it was sad to leave him locked in a cage all day. One day, I decided to let him go free in the forest. I watched him jump into the trees, and as he moved about, I could see all the natural feelings and instincts in him surge almost immediately to the surface. His original nature had never been lost or relinquished.

PEOPLE ARE SLOW LEARNERS

Chang T'ung and Chao Fu both became apprentices in Chinese medicine under the same doctor. They spent most of their formative years together, and consequently, the two became very good friends.

When they took up practicing medicine on their own, the two worked in different villages, but their homes were actually quite close to each other. The two men saw each other often, and after they started families, their wives and children also became good friends with one another. Relations between the two families were so good that even their dogs became friends. The two animals often played together.

Then one day, some insignificant little incident caused a difference of opinion to develop between the two families. An argument ensued, and feelings got hurt. Then both families went their separate ways and completely stopped seeing each other.

Two years slipped by with no one from either home talking to anyone from the other. No one was mad any longer, but no one in either family wanted to lose face by being the first to apologize.

The people in both families maintained their proud silences, but their dogs knew nothing of feelings like that. The two animals continued to visit each other and play with each other day after day.

Then one evening, under an expansive winter sky, the Chaos' dog, Hsiao Pai, came looking for the Changs' dog, Hsiao Hei. When Hsiao Pai found Hsiao Hei, he noticed that Hsiao Hei had a cut on his side that was bleeding. Without further delay, Hsiao Pai started to lick the cut clean.

The instinctive, unadorned, unselfish affection the dogs displayed toward each other at that moment was so conspicuous that even a human being could not fail to notice it.

When Chang T'ung saw the dogs together, he experienced an awakening shock of guilt and remorse. He said to his wife, "Look at that! These dogs are better creatures than we are. They don't get puffed up with pride, and they don't spend years resenting things that never mattered anyway."

The next day, Chang took his entire family to go see the Chaos. Within moments of seeing each other again, all their cold feelings became warm, and the two families quickly became best of friends once more.

TRAFFIC STOP

One day, I found myself caught in rush hour traffic in Panch'iao, Taiwan. My car was first in line at a red light. In the rearview mirror, I could see a long line of cars waiting behind us. Just as the light changed, I noticed something moving out of the corner of my eye. I asked the driver not to go forward.

As I looked more closely, I saw six little puppies trying to cross the road in front of us. They were turning their heads and looking all around. First they would watch the pedestrians strolling along, then they would sniff the air as if some wonderful odor were drifting by. They stopped and looked at our car. From the way they were looking at us, it seemed as if they were wondering why we had closed ourselves up a metal box when the weather outside was so beautiful.

People waiting behind us in line started becoming very impatient since we were not moving at all. Some of them started honking their horns and then some of them got out of their cars to come up front to see what was happening.

One pretty tough-looking guy came walking up between the cars. He turned his head toward us as if he were going to yell at us, but before he could speak, I smiled at him and pointed to the front. As soon as he saw the six little puppies in the road, he turned toward me and pressed his hands together to indicate he was sorry for having become angry.

The next people to come forward looking for someone to blame were a couple of young people dressed in punk fashions. When they saw the group of puppies walking along contentedly, so oblivious to the dangers around them, they both smiled. One of them knelt to watch the dogs, while the other went back to call their friends to come and look.

At last, the puppies made it to the other side of the street. When all the people who had gotten out of their cars to watch them saw that they were finally safe, they began applauding with relief. Just as we were getting ready to go again, the traffic light turned back to red. All around us people were laughing and talking as they returned to their cars.

RETURNING TO NATURE

Some years ago, a disciple gave a myna bird to Venerable Yi Yen. Yi Yen kept the bird in a cage outside her room. She named the bird "Ah Kuan."

Ah Kuan was no different from other myna birds. His feathers were black and shiny. Whenever he looked at people his eyes would move up and down as if he were scrutinizing them carefully. He was a good bird, but in the beginning there was nothing special about him. After a few months of Yi Yen's loving care, however, he began to develop some interesting abilities. Whenever anyone approached him, he would open up his wings and flap them back and forth. Then he would stretch his neck and say, "Amitabha! Amitabha!"

Before services, he often would puff up his chest and bravely announce, "Disciples and Dharma protectors! How are you? Welcome to Buddha's Light Mountain!" His pronunciation was perfect and the tone of his voice was as good as any radio announcer's.

During chanting services, we became accustomed to hearing him sing along with us. He really sang expressively and with a sensitive rhythm.

Everybody loved that bird, and no one ever passed his cage without stopping for a minute to visit with him.

Sadly, though, all good things must come to an end. One afternoon, Venerable Yi Yen discovered his cage was empty. She looked all over for him, before she heard the faint, but recognizable sounds of Ah Kuan saying, "Amitabha!, Amitabha!" Yi Yen raised her head and saw that the bird was high in a tree, nodding at her. It seemed as if he were saying good-bye because in a moment he spread his wings and flew away.

The loss of such a good bird was painful to everyone, but Yi Yen was inconsolable. Everyone tried to comfort her, but nothing helped. She was so sad she couldn't even eat. When I found out how badly she felt, I said to her, "A bird's original home is in nature. Ah Kuan is special and he can talk, but is it best that he talk only to us? Now he can preach the Dharma to creatures in nature, too. Isn't that wonderful? Remember the old saying, 'Though confined to a cage, the heart remembers its natural home.' We should be happy for Ah Kuan, not sad at all."

When Yi Yen heard that, her face finally lit up with a beautiful smile.

ADDING COLOR

My attendant, Yung Hui, shares my love of small animals. Since everyone knows this about her, people often give her baby birds that have fallen out of their nests or that have been injured in some other way. Under her tender care, even seriously injured birds regain their health and energy.

I started giving the birds in her nursery the monastic name of Man Fei (Full Flight). As more birds were brought in to Yung Hui to be cared for, we had to keep adding numbers to their names. Pretty soon, we had a Full Flight No. 1, Full Flight No. 2, Full Flight No. 3, and so on. They were lodged in all kinds of cages and could be heard singing and flapping around all day long.

One day I said to Yung Hui, "A bird is a creature of nature. It's time to let them all return to their natural home."

The next day, after a short ceremony, she reluctantly let the birds go free. Since we were afraid the newly released birds might have problems getting enough to eat, we scattered seeds for them in a rear garden. Before long, the birds became very punctual about feeding times and always appeared regularly to take their meals. One of the birds was especially endearing to me. Every morning and evening he would land by my window and look at me carefully as if he wanted to be sure I was okay.

One night, I returned to Buddha's Light Mountain very late from a trip to Europe, where I had been preaching the Dharma. Early the next morning, I awoke to the strange sounds of many birds singing near my room. I went out back to see where the sounds were coming from. In the garden, I discovered a large cage had been constructed for birds. I looked closer and saw that inside the cage there was a group of parrots whose feathers flashed vibrantly and colorfully as the birds jumped from place to place. I knew this had to be the work of Yung Hui. I called her to me and asked her to take the cage down and release all the birds. It was easy to see that she was very unwilling to do what I asked.

She did do it, though, and now the skies around Buddha's Light Mountain are filled with the vivid colors of parrots flying back and forth. One day I pointed to a flock of the colorful birds and said to her, "Look! Look how much color you have added to the monastery!"

She lifted her eyes to look where I was pointing. The sun coming through the trees dappled her face as she smiled at the sight of the birds soaring above us.

MAN TI RUNS AWAY

A South Pacific Typhoon was blowing hard outside again. Inside my room, I had a new guest—a little squirrel who had been blown out of the trees by the wind. He was nestled in a stack of towels inside a small box on a table. Someone had found him on the ground outside and brought him to me. His eyes had still not opened and his fur had not begun to grow yet. His naked little body was the tender color of flesh. He looked like a newborn baby. I had a light near him to keep him warm, and every four hours I gave him milk to drink. His little box must have been very much like the incubators human beings use to care for premature babies. There was a problem, however. This little squirrel was not like other ones I had cared for. Every time he swallowed a mouthful or two of milk, he would quickly vomit it back up again. While he was vomiting, a small stream of blood would flow from his little nose. I wondered if he had not suffered an internal injury in his fall from his nest. I wanted to take him to a veterinarian, but the storm outside was peaking and there was no way we could go out in it.

I had to do the best I could with what I had available. I put a tiny portion of antibiotic powder in some water. Then, as I recited the Buddha's name, I pried open his little mouth and forced him to swallow some of the stuff. Thanks to the mercy of Buddha, on the next day the little squirrel began to look a little better. From then on he became a source of deep concern for everyone around him.

I've taken care of many little squirrels who have fallen from their nests. I always give them the monastic name Man Ti (Full Land). A number usually follows the name, but since I had had so many squirrels, I couldn't remember what number was supposed to come after this new one. All I could do was call him Full Land No. N.

Probably because we had cared for him so much, Full Land No. N was much more friendly with people than any other squirrel I had ever nursed back to health. After a few months, he grew a beautiful coat of fur and had a thick tail which he flicked around like a Chinese fan. His teeth were sharp as knives and his claws could scratch like needles. Whenever he climbed on our furniture, he would leave behind small marks where he had gnawed and scraped the wood. However, whenever he jumped on our laps or crawled across our heads, he was always careful to move gently as if he were afraid of hurting us. He followed us up and down stairs and would quickly jump onto a hand offered to him. Sometimes he would race ahead of us as we walked. He was a great little friend and a wonderful addition to the monastery.

After ten months like this, Full Land No. N was old enough to be sent back to nature, so one day we took him to a garden out back to let him go. When we released him we were afraid he might not want to leave, so we quickly went back inside to leave him by himself. After a while we pulled back the corner of a window shade to peek outside. There he was, still standing in the place we had left him. . .

From then on, we would frequently hear the little voice of Full Land No. N chattering outside. He fell into the habit of coming around several times a day to see us. After a few months, however, he gradually stopped coming by so often. Finally, we lost touch with him altogether.

Then one day I heard his familiar chattering outside again. I opened the door to look, and there was Full Land No. N. As soon as he saw me, he blinked his eyes and swept his tail back and forth. Standing right beside him was a beautiful female squirrel. After a long moment, Full Land No. N turned, and with his companion, ran back into the trees. As the two of them ran away, I knew he had come to see me for the sole purpose of reporting his good news.

LIVING WITH A SNAKE

Some years ago, Venerable Hsin Ting returned to his room to change his robe after morning chanting services. When he opened his closet, he was surprised to see something curled in the shadows. Hsin Ting turned on the light and bent to examine the form more closely. In the corner of his closet, he saw a python curled and waiting. The snake raised its head and sampled the air with its tongue.

Hsin Ting smiled and greeted the snake cheerfully. "Do you like it here?" he asked. "If you want to stay here, you are more than welcome, but please, let's follow a few rules: you don't bother me and I won't bother you. How does that sound?"

The snake slowly lowered its head and calmly lay still as if it had understood what Hsin Ting had said to it.

From then on, Hsin Ting always made sure to greet the snake when he came into his room and to say good-bye to it when he left. In response, the snake would always raise his head and then settle down again. The two of them lived peacefully and quietly like that for over a month.

Then, one day Hsin Ting returned to his room only to find that the python had disappeared. In the place where the snake had slept, however, it had left a long coil of snake skin almost as if it were trying to say good-bye.

Hsin Ting has told this story quite a few times, and whenever he gets to the end, he always says, "You know, if I can make a snake listen to me, just think what I will be able to accomplish with people!"

BLACK TIGER

About ten years ago, Great Compassion Nursery School at Buddha's Light Mountain had a dog called Black Tiger. Black Tiger was a good name for the dog because his fur was pitch black, his face looked like a tiger's, and his bark was loud and forthright. The problem with Black Tiger was he was too good at being a guard dog. Nothing escaped his notice. Just about everything that moved caused him to bark loudly. Before long, he began to irritate the old people who were at Buddha's Light Mountain. Eventually, they said that if Black Tiger were not sent away, they would report us to the newspapers and say we were not caring for them properly.

An old Chinese saying describes the problem well: "The good door is hard to open, and good deeds are hard to do." The old people complained about Black Tiger so much that many of the monastics became concerned they really might try to cause us some trouble.

No matter what kind of situation I am in, I always try to do what is right without worrying about whether I will be blamed or praised, or whether I will gain or lose by what I do. I had to think of some way to solve the problem of Black Tiger without hurting anyone's feelings. Finally, I asked Venerable Hui Ting of Ch'ao Yuan Temple in Mei Nung to take the dog. At the same time, I acquired a much gentler dog to replace Black Tiger at the nursery school to avoid causing the children there any unhappiness at losing their companion. This solution seemed to please both the old folks and the children, and the matter ended there.

Over the ensuing months, however, I often heard stories about Black Tiger and how he would be especially friendly to anyone who had just come from Buddha's Light Mountain. It seemed as if he still remembered us and was missing us. I felt sad to hear that about Black Tiger, but I also felt it was hard to believe he was really acting the way people said he was. I wanted to go see him, but I was too busy to find the time.

Eight years slipped by before I found the chance to go to Ch'ao Yuan Temple for a visit. Black Tiger still remembered me. He wasn't angry with me at all. Instead, he ran all over the yard, twisting his body, as he turned circles around me. He stayed by my side the whole time I was at the temple, clearly expressing his long-remembered affection for me. To see with my own eyes how much he still remembered me and cared for me was very, very moving. We had sent him over one hundred miles away from us, but deep in his heart, he had never left us at all.

Stories About

MONASTICS

THE CAR

In 1985 while Venerable Hui Lung was abbot of Lei Yin Temple in Ilan, Taiwan, the temple conducted a seven-day Amitabha retreat. Devotees from all over Taiwan came to attend the retreat.

When the seven days were over and everyone had gone, Hui Lung discovered that a car had been left parked outside the temple. The car was an old sedan, and when no one came to claim it after a few days, Hui Lung began to worry that the car would deteriorate if no one cared for it. Accordingly, Hui Lung dusted the car off and kept it clean and ran the engine for a while once a day. He fell into the habit of doing that every day, and before long, four years passed.

Then one day, a man named Tu Tsung-liang came to Ilan on business. As Tu passed the temple, he was astonished to see that the car parked out front looked a lot like his old car. "Can that be my old car?" he asked himself.

Tu went into the temple to inquire about the car. It turned out that Tu had lent his car to a friend during the retreat four years before, and then had forgotten where his friend had said he had parked it. When Tu couldn't find the car, he assumed it had been stolen, and gave it up as lost.

Tu was delighted to see his old car, and when he got in the driver's seat and started the engine, he discovered it was running even better than it had been before. Tu was so grateful to have his old car back, he decided on the spot to order a new car and donate it to the temple. That night, he drove the old one back home with him.

LOOKING FOR A HOME
OUTSIDE OF HOME

Hsiao Chun strolled into Buddha Hall curiously looking all around. Smoke from burning incense swirled slowly in the dim light coming in through the windows. The master in charge of incense and oil lamps turned away from the altar and walked toward the young boy.

"My young friend," he said smiling, "have you come to bow to Buddha?"

"Master!" the boy said, "I found one yuan outside! Can I put it in the donation box?"

"What a kind thought," the incense master said. "Kindness like yours one day will carry you all the way to Buddhahood."

The incense master rubbed the boy's head as he gently directed him to the ochre donation box where he could make his small offering. The boy placed his money in the slot, and then burst into smiles and laughed. Then he turned and ran home.

The next day, the boy came again. When he saw the incense master he called out, "Master! I found another yuan. Can I donate this one, too?"

The boy was full of sincerity and enthusiasm, and the incense master smiled at him with his whole heart. "Of course you can donate it," he said. "Would you like to take some of this candy which has been left before the Buddha? It will make you strong and wise."

The day after that, the little boy came again, and again he said that he had found a one-yuan coin outside the temple. This time the incense master thought it was a little strange so he asked the boy, "Where do you keep finding all this money you're bringing here?"

For the first time, Hsiao Chun acted timid and shy. "The truth is," he said, "I didn't find this money. It's mine. When I came here the first day, I noticed that you were kind and gentle. I wanted to talk to you and I wanted to be with you again. It's not like my home here at all. At home, all I ever hear is my parents arguing with each other. When they don't argue with each other, they complain about me.

"In school my teachers just judge me on my grades, and nothing else.

It's only when I'm here with you, Master, that I feel like a real person. Just to hear the sound of your voice makes me feel happy again."

The incense master touched the boy's head and smiled. "You don't have to bring any money to come here and see me," he said. "You can come here any time you want. I will always be happy to see you!"

This story should be a small warning to all parents. Don't make your home so miserable your children have to look for a home outside of home.

STRENGTH AND FAITH

In 1961, at the end of a Buddhist service in Huwei, Taiwan, Venerable Yi Miao came up to me to talk. Her manner was solemn. She said, "I'm afraid I will never see you again. . . . I have cancer and my doctor says I will not live more than another month or two."

I was very young at the time. I felt badly for her, but I really didn't know what to say to comfort her. "Monastics should look upon life and death as nothing," I said. "We just live one day at a time. Keep doing whatever you can to help others and don't worry about anything else."

I didn't realize it at the time, but she took those words to heart. Soon she got over her gloomy mood and started working as an announcer for a Buddhist radio program. To support the program, she spent most of her remaining time raising money for the station. The next time I saw her, her face was flushed with healthful color.

It's been over twenty years now, and her program "The Voice of Buddhism" still is encouraging her listeners to be strong and have faith, just as her life has been an example of strength and faith.

LENDING MONEY

One hot afternoon a few years ago, just as Venerable Tz'u Hui was going in the front door of Universal Gate Temple, a young boy with a heavy backpack full of books ran up to her. With his hat clutched tightly in his hand, he asked her, "Master! My mom's not home! Can I borrow a hundred yuan?"

For a second Tz'u Hui felt a little suspicious. She thought to herself, "How is it that kids these days just go up to anybody to ask for money?" Then she looked more closely at the boy. His face was red with exertion. Beads of sweat covered his brow, and he seemed to be waiting for her reply with real anxiety. She decided he probably really needed the money, so she reached into her wallet and pulled out one hundred yuan to give to him.

Tz'u Hui forgot about the incident until more than a month later. She was waiting for the elevator to go up to Universal Gate Temple when she heard a voice whispering behind her.

"Look carefully, now. Which one was it?"

"Mom! She's the one! Right there!"

Tz'u Hui turned to look at the boy, and saw that he was pointing at her. The boy's mother rushed forward and grabbed Tz'u Hui's hand. "Master," she said, "I am so grateful to you! Over a month ago we had a little accident at our home. I couldn't get to school to pick up my son on time, so he left on his own. Thank goodness he found you! It was so kind of you to lend him one hundred yuan so he could get something to eat and take the bus home. Thank you!"

When she finished speaking, she pulled a packet of money out of her pocket and stuck it into Tz'u Hui's hand. "Please be kind enough to accept this money. Allow my family to plant some good karmic seeds with it."

When Tz'u Hui opened the packet later on, she discovered there was one hundred thousand yuan inside.

TWO NUNS AND THEIR
LITTLE GUEST

One day, while Venerable Tz'u Hui and Venerable Tz'u Chia were in Japan, they decided to have some Japanese food for lunch. They went into a narrow sushi bar and took a small table near the back of the room. At the table next to them was a young couple who were speaking together so earnestly, they all but forgot their young son who was with them.

The boy was five or six years old and full of life. With no one paying attention to him, his innate curiosity started him roaming around the restaurant to look for something to do. From time to time he would drift up to the nuns' table and smile or make a face at them, and then run away.

When the sushi the nuns had ordered was placed on their table, the boy appeared again. With an inquisitive frown on his face, he poked his head over the edge of the table to see what was there. Then suddenly he reached out one of his small hands and grabbed a piece of sushi from their plate.

The boy immediately stuck the food in his mouth and then opened his two eyes wide to see what reaction he would draw from the nuns. Tz'u Chia only looked at him placidly and nodded her head and smiled.

When the boy saw how friendly she was being, he reached out again and took another piece of sushi from their plate. By this time everyone in the restaurant, except the boy's parents, was aware of what was happening. With a sense of amused interest, they all turned to watch the drama of "The Two Nuns and Their Little Guest" as it continued to unfold. When the child noticed that everyone was watching him, he threw himself into his part with redoubled vigor. He grabbed piece after piece of sushi from the nuns' plate and crammed them into his mouth.

Before long almost all of the sushi was gone. Just as he was getting to the last few pieces, the boy's parents suddenly noticed what their son was doing. In a glance, they realized that the whole restaurant was watching him take food off the nuns' table. His mother blushed to the roots of her hair and, bowing as she rose from her chair, apologized profusely to Tz'u Hui and Tz'u Chia for what her son had done. At the same time, she managed to grab her son by the ear and give it a mighty twist. Then her other hand rose in the air in preparation to strike the boy on the side of his head for his misdeeds.

"Please don't hit him!" Tz'u Chia cried out. "We've been happy to give him that food. It's been a way for us to form a friendship with him. He's done nothing wrong."

With those words, the boy's young mother relaxed somewhat. She continued to apologize to the nuns for what had happened, but since no one was angry, she abandoned the idea of disciplining her boy and only gently led him back to their table by his hand.

With their food all but gone, Tz'u Hui and Tz'u Chia had little left to do but rise from their table and pay their bill. They didn't get very much to eat that day, but the pleasure of seeing the little boy and forming a friendship with him left a "taste" in their hearts richer and better than any sushi they could have had.

A NUN'S HEART

When we first opened Great Compassion Nursery School at Buddha's Light Mountain, we were really short of help. When Venerable Yi Hung, who had been a nun for over ten years, saw how acute the school's need was, she immediately volunteered to work with the children.

She was very steady and dedicated in her work. One day, however, I suddenly realized that I hadn't seen her around for quite some time. She wasn't coming to the dining hall for her meals anymore, and I never saw her walking around the grounds, as I had gotten used to. I became worried about her and asked where she was.

I was told that there had been an outbreak of chickenpox at the nursery school, and that to prevent the disease from spreading, the children had been quarantined in one room of the school. Yi Hung had volunteered to stay with them night and day to take care of all their needs. She cooked for the children, gave them their medicines, read stories to them, and comforted them in any way she could think of.

As people learned about how hard she was working to make the children feel at ease, many complimented her quite openly. Others, though, seemed not to understand very well why she was doing what she did. "They're just a bunch of children," they said. "When they grow up, there's no guarantee they will stay around here anyway. Why do you go to all this trouble just for them?"

She answered, "These children are here precisely because they have no parents of their own. Buddhism itself has become their mother and father. I am merely participating in that."

Other people observed how deeply the children loved her and how closely they followed her. They asked her, "You've never been a mother, how is it you are able to raise these children so well?"

Yi Hung answered simply, "You don't have to have children to learn how to be a parent. You just have to fully express your inner love and compassion; then all the world will be your child."

A THIEF IN CH'AN HALL

Soon after a young man came to stay at Ch'an Hall, the other residents began noticing that things were being stolen. It was quite clear who the thief was, and suggestions were made to him, but nothing changed; he continued to take things that did not belong to him. The residents at the hall complained to the monk in charge about the young man, but all that the monk did was mumble a few syllables in response while taking no action against the young thief.

Things went on like that for a while longer. Then some of the residents again went to the monk to complain about the thief. As he had before, the monk merely mumbled toward them, as he nodded his head. In the end, he took no action at all.

At last, everyone became so upset at the thief, and now at the monk, that they all went in a group to the monk's office to demand that he send the thief away. "If you don't send him away from here, we are going to leave this place ourselves!"

The monk looked at them for a moment. Then he replied in a very mild tone of voice: "If all of you leave, that will be too bad; but the truth is, if I have to choose between all of you and him, I would rather see you leave than him. You see, if all of you leave, there will be nothing to worry about. You all know how to take care of yourselves and you all know how to control your behavior. If he leaves, however, I really don't know what will happen. If we can't tolerate him here, what will happen when he is out in the world? He might become even worse than he is here. He might bring lots of harm to society. I appeal to your social consciences; let him stay here with us until he sees the light for himself and changes of his own accord."

After hearing the monk speak, the residents felt more than a little ashamed of themselves. They agreed to control their anger and say nothing more about the thief.

Unknown to everyone at the time, the thief himself had been eavesdropping on them since the moment they had gathered in the room to speak to the monk. When the thief heard what transpired on his account, he became so ashamed of himself, he broke into tears and swore he would never steal again. From that day on, he worked very hard at practicing Buddhism. Eventually, he took monastic vows and became Venerable Pa Fang.

THE PURE LAND

Venerable Hsin Ting, who has dedicated his life to helping all sentient beings, is a very popular monk. He is frequently asked to visit branch temples all over Taiwan to preach the Dharma. Hsin Ting always does his best to keep up with the needs of the faithful, so he spends a good part of his time traveling back and forth across Taiwan.

A young boy used to visit Universal Gate Temple in Taipei with his mother quite regularly. He had the chance to hear Hsin Ting speak more than a few times, and he came to admire him very much. Once, the boy told a friend of his, "Master Ting teaches us to sing and chant and meditate, but I like the way he smiles best of all!"

One day, the boy became seriously ill and had to be sent to the hospital. His illness caused him to suffer and lose a lot of weight. The boy pleaded with his mother, "Mom! I want to see Master Ting! Mom! Master Ting is so compassionate, don't you think he would come see me if I asked him to?"

Before long, Hsin Ting heard about the boy's illness and about his desire to have him come to the hospital to see him. The monk left immediately to go see the boy. When he arrived, he heard the boy tell his mother,

"Mom, you've always taught me that when I die Amitabha Buddha will take me to the Pure Land if I chant his name often in this life. Well, look what happened! I said Master Ting's name over and over and he has come to see me. Now I understand that I don't have to die to go to the Pure Land. I am so happy right now. I know Master Ting has brought the Pure Land to me here!"

GIVING OTHERS JOY

Most of the monastics from Buddha's Light Mountain who preach the Dharma in Hong Kong are natives of Taiwan. They always learn some Cantonese (the dialect spoken in Hong Kong), but generally they never feel quite as much at home with Cantonese as they do with Taiwanese. Hong Kong is part of China, but the language and the culture can be quite different from Taiwan.

One day, a group of monastics decided to go to an old people's retirement home in Hong Kong to visit with the residents. After they had been there for some time, the monastics noticed that their presence was doing little or nothing to lift the residents out of what appeared to be a very gloomy and lonely mood. It seemed as if they were being completely unsuccessful in bringing joy and happiness into the retirement home.

As the mood of the monastics slowly began to sink to the gloomy level of the residents, the leader of their group said quietly, "Remember, we are only here to bring happiness to others. We should not even think about whether they are giving us happiness or not."

With that advice, the monastics' energy was renewed, and they continued working with the residents for some time longer. When the group finally was getting ready to leave, one old man grabbed hold of one of the monk's hands, and without letting go said, "I've been here a long time, but this is the first time I've ever seen a group of Buddhist monks come to visit. I can't tell you how happy it has made me to have you all come here today. This little present is for you. Please accept it as a small token of my gratitude."

Without waiting for him to respond, the old man turned and left the monk holding the package all alone. Only after the group of monastics had returned to their temple did the monk open the bag the old man had given to him. Inside he found a loose pile of cash, and buried in the bills, a single, shining piece of gold. The recognition and kindness represented by the gold and the pile of bills had the effect of immediately lifting everyone's spirits. One young nun said, "So, in the end it was not we who brought them joy, but they who brought us joy!"

I'LL TAKE THAT ON MYSELF

In the early 1980s, Venerable Hui Lung was driving a compact car in the mountains on his way back to Buddha's Light Mountain when he crashed into a tractor driven by a farmer who had no license to drive. Neither the farmer nor the tractor were hurt in the crash, but Hui Lung was seriously injured.

Hui Lung's car was badly crushed and when the farmer looked inside, he saw that Hui Lung, who was slumped in his seat, was bleeding profusely from cuts on his head. The farmer knew that if he failed to act quickly, Hui Lung would not live long. Luckily, he succeeded in finding someone to take them to a hospital where emergency procedures saved the monk's life.

When Hui Lung had finally passed the danger point, the emergency room doctor came out to the waiting room and told the farmer, "He has broken eight bones in his arms and ribs. He will have to stay in the hospital for at least three months for treatment."

When he heard this news, the farmer felt terrible because he knew there was no way he could afford to pay such a large bill. At the same time, he felt responsible for what had happened to Hui Lung. He went to Hui Lung's bedside to explain how he felt and to apologize for being too poor to help Hui Lung in the way he knew he should.

From his bed, the monk turned the farmer's apology into an opportunity to comfort him, "Don't worry about the money," he said. "I don't even want you to pay it. That accident was my karma and I will endure the consequences of it myself."

MY FATHER

Venerable Yi Ch'eng was an outreach worker for the health clinic at Buddha's Light Mountain. As part of her job, she often went with the clinic van deep into the mountains to bring medical supplies and assistance to those who might not otherwise have a chance to receive them. Her work was satisfying and useful, and Yi Ch'eng was happy to be doing it.

Then one day, Yi Ch'eng learned that her father had come down with a serious illness. Yi Ch'eng immediately had her father brought to Buddha's Light Mountain where she could care for him personally. She quit traveling with the clinic van, and instead spent her time caring for her father's every need. Every day she washed him, changed his clothes, fed him, shaved him and comforted him in every way she could. Yi Ch'eng came from a large family, but not one of her brothers or sisters ever so much as came to Buddha's Light Mountain to visit their father, let alone help Yi Ch'eng with caring for him. Yi Ch'eng kept on like that for more than ten years, and no one ever heard her complain.

Once, a disciple gave me a box of peaches. I distributed the peaches to a group of monastics who happened to be nearby. Everyone ate their peach right away. Yi Ch'eng, however, did not eat hers. Instead, she simply held it quietly in her hand. Tz'u Hui, who was standing next to her, asked her why she was not eating her peach like everyone else.

Yi Ch'eng answered, "This peach is very special because Master Hsing Yun has given it to me. I want to save it for my father."

YOU'RE THE ONLY ONE

In the 1950s, few people in Taiwan had a good understanding of Buddhism. Most of them thought it was just superstition.

When Venerable Tz'u Jung decided to become a Buddhist nun, her family behaved as many would have at that time: they adamantly opposed her decision. Her older brother, especially, was against her becoming a nun. Her brother was a college graduate and the captain of a ship that sailed all over the world. He had had a lot of exposure to Western culture, so he was extremely impatient with Tz'u Jung's desire to dedicate her life to something he didn't think was worth anything at all.

"Buddhists are entirely useless. If you become a Buddhist nun, consider yourself out of this family. Don't even bother to ask how we are doing ever again."

Many years later, Tz'u Jung's mother became seriously ill. Since her children had scattered to places all over the world, there was no one who was able to take on the responsibility of caring for her—except Tz'u Jung.

Tz'u Jung, who was the abbess of Universal Gate Temple at the time, had her mother moved to a room in the temple so that she could care for her herself. Every morning and evening, she made time to go to her mother's bedside to comfort her and give her her medicines. Tz'u Jung cared for her mother like that until the old woman finally passed away.

One day the same brother who had spoken so harshly to her before came up to her and said, "There are eleven children in our family, and now it has turned out that of all of us, you are the only one who has been of any real use to our mother."

PLANTING SEEDS FOR HER SON

Once Venerable Tz'u Hui went to Hong Kong to preach the Dharma. After getting in a cab at the airport, she discovered that her driver was a rather talkative and pleasant woman.

"Master, where are you going?" the cab driver asked.

"To Fo Hsiang Lecture Hall," Tz'u Hui replied.

"Oh, Fo Hsiang Lecture Hall! Why that's part of Master Hsing Yun's Buddha's Light Mountain, isn't it?" The woman turned her head toward Tz'u Hui and presented her question as if she intended it to be a topic of conversation.

The sound of the car's tires hummed under them as city scenes sped past the window. The two women fell to talking together.

When the subject of taxi cabs in Hong Kong came up, the driver of the cab said, "My son is in Canada studying for his Ph.D. The cost of the degree is unbelievable! I have no choice but to come out here to earn extra money so he can concentrate on his studies and finish school without having to borrow too much."

As they drove, the woman talked on about how difficult it was for her family to make it economically and how hard they had to work to put their son through school.

The taxi slowed as it neared Fo Hsiang Lecture Hall. Tz'u Hui glanced at the meter and then added a large tip to the money she took out of her wallet to give the driver. Tz'u Hui wanted to show her support for this woman who would sacrifice so much just to help her son advance in the world. When the cab stopped, Tz'u Hui was surprised when suddenly the driver turned to her and handed her five hundred Hong Kong dollars.

"Please donate this money to Buddha for me," the woman said as she pressed the money into Tz'u Hui's hands. "And please pray that my son will get his degree quickly. I don't want to take any money from you at all. Please keep the taxi fare. Take it as a good seed I am planting for my son. I hope you understand what I am saying and that you will receive this small donation from me with pleasure."

Tz'u Hui could not refuse the sincerity and enthusiasm of the woman's gesture. As she left the cab and walked toward the hall, her heart was filled with admiration for this mother's devotion to Buddhism, as well as her devotion to her son.

LOST IN TIBET

To Venerable Man Hsueh, who grew up in the United States, Tibet was a land shrouded in mystery and wonder.

In 1994, Man Hsueh was chosen to lead a group of American students from Hsi Lai Temple on a tour of Tibet. The trip proceeded like a dream, and by the time Man Hsueh finally landed in Tibet, she was almost dizzy with excitement.

Everything went more or less as planned until the third day when Man

Hsueh and her group became hopelessly lost during a walk in the hills near where they were staying. They turned down one path after another, but the group could find nothing familiar and no signs of any human life. The landscape around them became forbidding as the huge sky above them slowly grew darker.

Just as everyone was starting to become really afraid, they heard the footsteps of a young Tibetan man walking toward them. The man spoke halting Chinese, but he was able to communicate pretty well. After learning of their problem, he said, "It is very easy to become lost here. If you don't know this area well, you won't be able to find your way. Please wait here, while I go home to get my daughter. Then I will come back and take you to your hotel."

About ten minutes later, the young man returned. In his arms he held a small girl who looked to be about five or six years old. With the little girl in his arms, the young man led Man Hsueh and her group for over two hours. At last they arrived back at their hotel. Everybody was exhausted by the long journey through the moonlight. They were all glad to go inside the hotel.

In the dim light of the building's small lobby, Man Hsueh and her group noticed for the first time that the young man who had guided them out of the hills had been carrying his daughter in his arms because the girl was crippled and unable to walk.

"This poor guy must be exhausted!" the members of the group began to say as soon as they had relaxed enough to appreciate how much he had done for them. Everyone began looking around for some things to give him for having helped them so much. The young man, however, refused everything that was offered to him except one small image of Avalokiteshvara that Man Hsueh presented to him.

"Thank you all for having given me this chance to be of service to you," he said quietly.

Then he hoisted his daughter back up into his arms and turned to begin the long walk back to his home.

BROTHERHOOD

Fang Hsi-sheng was a student at an agricultural institute in Taiwan. His brother was a monk at Buddha's Light Mountain. One day, the two of them were sitting around talking when Hsi-sheng said he would like to get a bicycle because he was tired of walking everywhere. The subject of their discussion moved on from there, and Hsi-sheng never thought about it again.

A month later, however, as Hsi-sheng was returning to his dorm at school, he heard someone call his name. When he turned to look for who it was, he saw his brother riding toward him on a new bicycle. His brother was smiling, and as he glided nearer, Hsi-sheng could see that his face was covered with perspiration.

Hsi-sheng was surprised to see his brother on a new bicycle, and he did not know what to say for a moment. Then he asked, "This must have cost you at least a couple thousand yuan. I know your allowance is only a couple hundred a month. How did you manage to buy it?"

"Let's just say I managed," Hui Lung answered. Then he continued, "I want to leave this bike here with you. It's a gift for you because you are my brother. I hope that you will use it often to ride up the mountain to visit me."

Life went on as usual for a few more years. Then one day Hsi-sheng rode his bicycle into the monastery, shaved his head, and became a monk named Hui Ch'uan.

DESERVING THEIR FAME

In 1967, I heard that an old people's home which was run by a Christian group was going to have to close due to lack of funds. That was just when we were starting to build Buddha's Light Mountain. Money was very short, but I felt I had to do something to help so we agreed to take over the old people's home. I know we solved a lot of problems for a lot of old people by making that decision. But we also caused ourselves some problems, too. The old people in the home came from many different backgrounds, and they all had different needs and expectations. No matter what you did, there would be many complaints. Many dedicated people vowed to go to the home and do their best, but within a few days they were usually driven right back out of there.

Pretty soon, no one wanted to go work there. One day, I brought up the problem before a group of monastics. Venerables Yi Jung and Shao Chueh raised their hands to volunteer to work at the home. All they did was raise their hands, but that gesture turned into a vow which has lasted thirty years. They are still there today, cooking and caring for the old people. They take them to the hospital when necessary and they chant sutras for them whenever someone dies. They have shown enormous patience and dedication in their work, and for this reason they have been chosen many times to receive the government sponsored prize, "Good People Doing Good Things."

They deserve their fame. Think about it: over half their lives have been spent in dedicated service to old people. If their hearts were not full to the brim with compassion and caring, how could they ever have succeeded in that?

WARMTH AND KINDNESS IN ANOTHER LAND

About ten years ago, a group of five of us landed at Haneda Airport in Japan. After passing through customs, we went into downtown Tokyo. We were looking for something to eat, but we could not find a single vegetarian restaurant. From time to time we would come across a place that said it served vegetarian food, but on closer examination, we always found they were using fish and garlic and onions, none of which we could eat. Their concept of vegetarian food was not the same as ours, and we had no choice but to continue looking.

We walked around for quite some time. By the time it started to get dark, we were all so famished our stomachs were growling. Finally, I suggested that we just buy some noodles and make them ourselves. Everyone thought that would be a good idea. Venerable Yi Chieh said, "As I remember, there is a place that sells noodles only a couple of blocks from here."

When she said that, it felt as if a rainbow had appeared in the clouds. Our energies were renewed, and we walked quickly to where we thought we would find those noodles for sale. When we got to our destination, we discovered a long line of people waiting to buy something from a middle-aged woman who was standing behind a counter. We looked at the sign over her store. None of us was sure what it said, but it was clear that she was not selling noodles. We stood around for a few minutes wondering what to do next. When the woman who ran the shop noticed that we were monastics, she bowed and asked us what we were doing. After we told her, she waved her hands in the air and said, "There is no noodle shop around here. If you want to get some noodles, you will have to go to the alley behind that street over there."

She spent quite a lot of time giving us detailed directions to the noodle shop. With the long line of people waiting beside us, we felt a little embarrassed and left quickly after her description.

We looked for the shop she had told us about, but we couldn't find it. Before long, we found ourselves back in front of her store again. Just as before, there was a long line of people waiting to do business with the woman inside. When she saw that we had come back empty-handed, she knew, without our saying anything, that we had failed to find the noodle shop.

Just as we were going to ask her again where the shop was, she announced in a loud voice, "I'm very sorry! I have to close now. I'm sorry to have kept you waiting for nothing. Please come back tomorrow." With that, all her customers left.

Then she came out, locked the door to her store, and led us to a noodle shop about fifteen minutes away. As we sat comfortably at our table, each of us holding a warm bowl of noodles, I looked out the window and watched the cold wind sweeping the streets outside. We were in a foreign country, but all of us could feel the warmth and kindness that surrounded us.

Where Is Your Buddha Nature?

Above: Transmitting the leadership of Fo Guang Shan to Venerable Hsin Ping in 1985.

Above left: Master Hsing Yun in his twenties.

Left and below: Surveying the land for the construction of Buddha's Light Mountain in 1967.

Right: Master Hsing Yun with his family in 1989.

Below: Master Hsing Yun at Lei Yin Temple in Taiwan, which he presided over from 1953 to 1962.

Right: Ch'i Hsia Shan Monastery in Jiangsu Province, China, where master Hsing Yun studied as a boy.

GLOSSARY

Amitabha Buddha: The Buddha of "Boundless light." One of the most popular Buddha's in East Asia.

Ananda: (Sanskrit bliss) One of the Buddha's most important disciples.

BLIA: See Buddha's Light International Association.

bodhisattva: (Sanskrit enlightened being) 1) Anyone who is seeking Buddhahood. 2) A highly realized being who stands on the edge of nirvana but remains in this world to help others achieve enlightenment.

Buddha: (Sanskrit awakened one) There are innumerable Buddhas in the universe. Shakyamuni Buddha is the historical Buddha who taught the Dharma on earth. He is generally thought to have lived between the years 463-383 BC.

Buddha's Light International Association (BLIA): A world-wide Buddhist organization founded by Master Hsing Yun in 1992.

Buddha's Light Mountain: (Chinese Fo Guang Shan) The name of Master Hsing Yun's principal monastery. Founded May 16, 1967. It is near Kaohsiung, Taiwan.

Buddha nature: The enlightened essence of all things. All sentient beings have Buddha nature. It is hidden from our awareness by greed, anger, and ignorance.

Chih K'ai, Master: Master Chih K'ai was Master Hsing Yun's master. He lived between 1911-1981.

Dharma: (Sanskrit carrying, holding) The teachings of the Buddha which carry or hold the truth.

Iso, Master: (1394-1481) Master Iso, who appears in many Ch'an stories, was also a good painter. His nickname was "son of crazy clouds." He became a monk at the age of six.

Koya, Master: (903-972) A famous Japanese Pure Land Buddhist master.

Kuan Kung: A legendary Chinese protector of Buddhist temples.

Kuan Yin: (Sanskrit Avalokiteshvara "he who hears the sound of the world") Kuan Yin, who is usually depicted as a woman in Buddhist art, can manifest in any form before those who have called on him.

nine unclean aspects of a dead body, the contemplation of: This contemplation is used to overcome excessive sexual desire or excessive attachment to the things of this world. It is not intended to make us feel revolted, but only to help us control our passions.

Ryokan, Master: (1758-1831) Master Ryokan is remembered for having been a good poet and a good musician.

Sangha: (Sanskrit crowd) The community of Buddhist monks and nuns.

sentient being: All beings with awareness or the potential for awareness. The Buddha taught that eventually all sentient beings will achieve Buddhahood.

Shakyamuni Buddha: The Buddha of our world system. The historical Buddha who taught the Dharma on earth. He is generally thought to have lived between the years 463-383 BC.

sutra: (Sanskrit threads) That which is threaded together, the written records of the Buddha's teachings. Early sutras were sewn together.

Vihara: (Sanskrit "sojourning place") Residence for monks or nuns.

Yin Kuang, Master: (1862-1940) The thirteenth patriarch of the Pure Land school. He was a famous contemplative and an influential writer.

yuan: The basic Chinese currency unit. One US dollar equals approximately 20-30 yuan as they are figured in Taiwan.

The "weathermark" identifies this book as a production of Weatherhill, Inc., publishers of fine books on Asia and the Pacific. Editorial supervision; Jeffrey Hunter. Book and cover design; Liz Trovato. Production supervision; Bill Rose. Printed and bound by R.R. Donnelly, USA. The typeface used is Perpetua.